GONE the GOLDEN DREAM

Jan Markell

D0596673

BETHANY HOUSE PUBLISHERS
MINNEAPOLIS, MINNESOTA 55438
A Division of Bethany Fellowship, Inc.

Published by Bethany Fellowship, Inc.
6820 Auto Club Road, Minneapolis, Minnesota 55438

Printed in the United States of America

Library of Congress Cataloging in Publication Data

Markell, Jan, 1944-
  Gone the golden dream.

    1. Converts from Judaism—Biography. 2. Leshenotsky family.
3. Lessin family. I. Title.
BV2623.A1M37   248'.246   79-16718
ISBN 0-87123-049-6

"Unto him that loved us and washed us from our sins in his own blood." Joseph Aaron Lessin
Donald Lessin
Roy Lessin

Acknowledgement

Gratitude, though often deeply felt, is not too frequently expressed—particularly to those who are like ships passing in the night, whose brief but brilliant light penetrates the gloom of loneliness and despair.

There were many such individuals along the way who led me to an awareness of my need of the Savior. To those dear ones who encouraged me to "search the scriptures whether these things be so," I am indebted. I am thankful, too, for their long-suffering love towards me as I resisted and halted between two opinions.

My joyous appreciation must be expressed to the Gideons, International, for the Bible they placed in a Las Vegas hotel room; and to Mrs. Rose Arensmeier for her deep, intercessory prayer on behalf of my son Roy. And my sincere appreciation for the intercessory prayer from many saints of God who upheld my faith in the Messiah when trials and testings seemed to almost break my spirit.

Also to sons, Don and Roy; and to Miss Jan Markell who so skillfully assembled the information found here and turned it into this finished book.

Joseph Aaron Lessin
March, 1979

JAN MARKELL has been in Jewish evangelism in the Twin City area for over seven years. She travels widely, speaking on behalf of Jewish missions and advocating strong Christian support of the nation of Israel. She has authored many articles for Christian magazines and has written three other books: *Angels in the Camp, Somebody Love Me!* and *Peace Amidst the Pieces.*

Table of Contents

Chapter One
The Promised Land

Eliezer hurriedly stuffed the precious letter into his shirt. His mother was anxiously calling to him from behind their house.

"I'm on my way," he soothed her patiently. Eliezer couldn't get too excited about another Cossack raid. They had happened before and would happen again. On his way to join the family in the backyard shed, he glanced through the front room window to the end of the dirt street. Even from a block away, he could feel the ground shake beneath the house as the thundering raiders surged by, fortunately, on a cross street. The Leshenotsky family was probably safe—for this time.

Eliezer felt the letter crinkle inside his shirt as he sank to the wooden bench beneath the window. Pulling it out again, he felt the same wave of excitement as when he first opened it. He almost never received letters, and this one was from the Promised Land—America! His older brother Baruch was now living there.

Baruch, who had reluctantly left his wife and small son behind, told about his fruit-peddling job, from which he was carefully saving his earnings to bring his little family to America. And, he continued, he wanted to save enough so that Eliezer also could come! "This is a marvelous country," he wrote, "with many opportunities for work! And there is so much that one can buy with the money earned. I can't possibly describe it all to you. Our Russia is a much older nation; and yet this one, an infant in comparison, is so far ahead in every way."

Eliezer gazed out the window at the little village of Boyerker, the only home he had ever known. His expression hardened as he heard the Cossacks returning from their attack. He could picture in his mind the destruction left behind this pack of hungry wolves. Torches set to the flimsy, paintless shacks left them in smoldering ruins within minutes. Cattle were stolen or shot. The market area in the center of the village would be in shambles, the merchandise plundered or trampled under boots and hoofs. And now in the quiet after the storm, he heard the screams and cries, the curses and the prayers, finally dwindling to hopeless resignation.

Eliezer's sigh came out of the deep turmoil in his soul—the great love he had for his family, his home, his country, over against the despair he felt. The attack this morning was merely one small part of the Russian pogroms—the planned extermination of her Jews. Besides the pogroms, emigration and conscription were equally effective against the Hebrew minority; together they would result in the greatest modern-day exodus ever recorded.

At fifteen, Eliezer was a prime target for conscription. And that word meant almost certain death. Each week the Russian army stormed into the village to conscript Jewish men and boys (even as young as twelve). Russia needed a huge standing army because of her enormous border and her conflicts with China and Japan. But besides the necessarily huge army, conscription was a convenient method for killing more Jews: they were the first to be sent to the front lines of battle.

His reverie cut short by the deep voice of his father, Eliezer looked around to find the usual activity of the home resumed. The raid was over, the Leshenotskys had not this time suffered loss of life or property, and life went on.

"Come, Son, there is not time to sit dreaming over letters! We will have much work to do after the Cossacks' visit." Not that Father Leshenotsky in any way felt secret delight in the plight of his unfortunate neighbors, but he was well aware that there would be plenty of broken glass to be replaced by the Leshenotsky glaziers.

Bent almost in two under the weight of a large pane of glass, Eliezer joined his father in the street. Through the pall of smoke, already they could see and hear indications of repairing and rebuilding in the wake of today's raid. The "shtetl" of Boyerker, not far from Kiev, the capital of the Ukraine, might be bowed but she was not broken. The underlying strength of that indomitable Jewish spirit was hope of the coming Messiah. The orthodox among peasant Jewry pulled along the less devout and fainthearted with that small but intense light at the end of the tunnel.

"But," Eliezer thought as he followed his father in the direction of the morning's invasion, "I doubt that I can hold out that long. It is no less than a miracle that I have not yet been caught by the army's round-up or killed in a raid. My only hope is found in this letter." The letter almost burned against his chest.

Eliezer was so immersed in this dream that he hardly felt the broken glass cutting into his bare feet as he helped Ephraim measure and cut the replacement window at their first stop. There just was not enough money for shoes at this time. Eliezer's lack of shoes, though, would have been at the bottom if he had made a list of deprivations. For example, the youth within the shtetls had little, if any, childhood and little time for play. After all, there was work to be done, besides the extensive study of the Torah. So Eliezer was mature for his fifteen years. Since many of his friends, even those younger than he, had already been forced into the army, his few precious moments of free time were spent in dreaming of the future. And to Eliezer, the future meant America.

Did he dare discuss this dream with his father? Looking up into Ephraim's work-lined face, he could read the pain and disappointment with life in his eyes. But Eliezer knew also that part of his father's pain was caused by the oldest son's turning away from life in Boyerker and departure for America. Could Eliezer add to that pain? *Would* he add to it? Maybe the trailblazing done by Baruch would carry Eliezer over the dilemma.

"Baruch wants me to come to America," he began cautiously, hurrying to keep up with his father as they went to their next job. Ephraim was noted throughout the village for his strength. Eliezer saw him quicken his pace and knew that he was irritated.

Finally Ephraim answered, "America is a land where meat is unkosher and the Sabbath is not the Sabbath." Without turning around he continued, "It is corrupt and sinful and no place for a Jew! One Leshenotsky in America is enough."

"Father, no!" protested Eliezer, trying to balance the glass on his back and still look at Ephraim. "Baruch says it is a good place for Jews. He is saving his money, and some day he will send for Rivka, Rachmiel *and* me, if I would like. And, Father," he pleaded, "I *would* like to go."

What was it about America that so fired the imagination of the young men like Eliezer? Even as early as the 1800's, America was the "golden medineh," the golden dream for many Jewish youth in the land of the Czars. Actually, the dream probably began in earnest with the assassination on March 1, 1881, of Alexander II, Czar of Russia, by revolutionary terrorists.

Alexander II had eased considerably the pitiful condition of Russia's Jews. A ray of hope had come when he opened the doors of some universities to them and even allowed some educated Jews to hold public office. He had abolished conscription of Jewish children and given a new kind of freedom to a few Jewish businessmen and merchants. It had appeared to be a new day for the Jews of Eastern Europe.

But merely weeks after this assassination, the most vicious pogroms in Russia's history began. Eastern Europe's Jewish people were left stunned, bleeding and homeless. The new Czar, Alexander III, initiated policies that were devastating to Jews. They were forced to consider a new exodus. (Between 1881 and 1914, two million of them would emigrate to America, Palestine and other countries of the world. History showed this to be the highest rate of emigration in modern times.)

"You will all end up a burden on American charities," Ephraim said to the plea in his son's eyes. "Actually, there's probably no charity for Jews, even in America. Why should Americans treat Jews any differently than the Cossacks do?"

Eliezer hardly knew how to answer his father, but at least Ephraim hadn't yet closed the subject. "Well," he began slowly, "Baruch says America is a democracy, and that means that everybody gets treated the same . . . " He trailed to an uncertain stop.

Catching the uncertainty, Ephraim responded, "Everybody but the Jews, Son. It is that way in most countries." But this idea was in direct contradiction to the desperate Russian Jews who would save their rubles for years in order to buy a ticket to freedom—passage to America. Borrowing, pawning, scrimping, praying and even begging from relatives, they looked toward the Promised Land.

You see, Russia was the classical home of anti-Semitism. World Jewry had settled there in the sixteenth century, and for centuries Russia herded Jews away from the rest of her inhabitants lest they be "exploited" by them. Usually confined to the "Pale of Settlement," eventually 95% of the Russian Jewish population were limited to these "authorized" areas in the Ukraine, Poland, Lithuania and Byelorussia. Except for temporary periods when restrictions were eased, as under Alexander II, Russian Jews were either ignored or killed, with varying degrees of persecution between, depending on the pervading whim of the present rulers.

Granted, there were a few that served as Russia's leading merchants, traders and financiers, and others were found among the pioneers of the textile industry and railroad construction. But by far the largest portion of the Jewish population lived in the "shtetls"—the country villages found in the Pale that consisted of flimsy wooden houses clustered around a marketplace, and as crowded as a big-city slum.

Pitifully poor (the Russian peasant was the proprietor of at least a small piece of land, but not the Jews), members of the shtetl were considered "wretched refuse," locked into a poverty syndrome that was utterly without a solution as long as they lived among alien people.

This backward economy was a cultural incubator for Jewish traditions and values. In this shadowy existence they clung to one another for security, warmth and shelter. So Father Ephraim's suspicions were not without foundation. This dream of freedom to which young Jews clung seemed like an impossible fantasy to those whose life and history had known nothing but deprivations and persecutions.

"Baruch insists America is different!" Eliezer tried once more, as they passed the ravaged marketplace on their way to their next customer.

"So what does Baruch know? He is no world traveler. So he made it to America. Like I said, America is corrupt and no place for a Leshenotsky. If you want to leave Boyerker, you think about Palestine maybe. Not America."

And Eliezer knew that the subject was now closed—at least for a long time.

* * * * *

Coming back through the marketplace on their way home, Ephraim and Eliezer hardly noticed the men and women hovered over baskets of vegetables or eggs that somehow escaped destruction in the morning's raid. Hoping to sell their items before dark, they looked hopefully after the passing figures. The women, skin wrinkled and coarsened from years of exposure to sun and wind, wore scarves (babushkas) over their hair, even in the warm sun of a Ukrainian summer. Their long dark dresses were covered with colorful aprons. The men dressed all of a kind in simple trousers and jackets. Besides the long hours each day spent in earning a livelihood, they also set apart time every day for study of the Torah.

Ephraim pursed his lips in stubborn annoyance as he caught the word "America" and "golden medineh" in the babble of voices between market stalls. It could not be denied that among even those who had no intention of ever leaving the shtetl, America was a distant, magic land. Quarrels were quickly patched up so that letters from relatives and friends in the new land could be proudly shared. Everyone talked about America.

Passing the last stall, Eliezer caught a glimpse of a slender form, the setting sun burnishing her braids. Golda's parents had promised her to the Leshenotskys for their last son long before the youngsters would ever have thought of marriage. Eliezer still had never spoken to her, but he did on occasion catch her eye and make her blush. In this day of arranged marriages as had been done in Bible times, Eliezer was very glad that Golda was so lovely. He was sure that he could love her and that she could learn to love him.

"I wonder if Golda ever thinks about America," Eliezer mused to himself as they turned down their street for home and supper.

"How has our village fared this time?" queried Eliezer's mother as they all gathered around the simple wooden table for the evening meal.

"I don't think that the raid was as bad as the last one," Ephraim answered. "I believe that we'll be able to replace all the broken glass before the end of the week."

"The Cossacks left behind some of their wretched propaganda leaflets," Eliezer said hotly. "They are trying to humiliate us further by letting us see their anti-Jewish trash!" It was amazing how creative and imaginative the Russians could be in twisting events so that the Jews were the scapegoat for every failure—political or military. The press cooperated in this massive brainwashing program that set the Russian people against the Jews.

So Alexander III offered a solution to the "Jewish problem": one-third should be allowed to emigrate; one-third should convert to Christianity; and one-third should starve to death, be killed in battle, or be killed in the pogroms.

Noticing his youngest's preoccupation and downcast face, Ephraim was glad that his second two sons were settling into life here in Boyerker. Teve was already married and living in his own small house only a few blocks away. And Benyomin would be marrying very shortly. He had a job with a farmer just outside the outskirts of Boyerker and was able to come home almost every night. "And," Ephraim thought as he looked at his two daughters helping their mother to get the supper on the table, "both Hannah and Rachel are promised to steady, hard-working boys here in the village. I anticipate no problems there." Glancing over at Eliezer busy with his supper, Ephraim's thoughts continued, "He seems to have this crazy idea about America. That one I *am* worried about." Why couldn't Eliezer be content with life in Boyerker? So they had problems. The Leshenotskys had survived this long; they would continue to do so.

But Eliezer's dream only grew as the months and years rolled on. He watched with yearning heart as others from the village were finally able to save enough for the passage to America. The old ones shook their heads over the evening fire and prophesied no good for those who braved the terrors of the sea. The whole community turned out for the farewells at the train station. Loud weeping accompanied the good-byes, for who could be sure that a loved one would ever be seen again? Bewildered wives watched their husbands pull away from the station, already their hearts fixed on the day when enough money would be saved for their passage to join them. And for a few, that day would never come.

In 1910 Eliezer married Golda. Their wedding day was their first actual meeting. Ephraim helped the newlyweds find a cozy little house, and Golda settled right into making a home for them. Eliezer was still working with his father in the glazier business and Ephraim hoped that he had forgotten about America.

War clouds on the horizon in 1911 increased conscription activities. Eliezer had always managed to escape their random selection of soldiers. But this new round-up was making him very wary.

"I received a letter from Baruch," Eliezer slowly said to Golda as he came in from work one evening. Golda didn't answer, merely looking at him with questions in her eyes. "He has enough saved for one person to join him in America, and he thinks that if I am that one, the two of us together can make money faster to bring you and Rivka and Rachmiel over also."

"O Eliezer!" Golda cried, her heart in her voice. "Isn't there some other way? And with our child coming . . . " Her voice trailed off. Wiping her eyes with her apron, she went on hurriedly, "And how will Rivka ever accept the wait? That passage money should be for her."

"You are forgetting their son, Golda. There is money enough at this time for only one. But don't worry, nothing is decided for sure yet. We'll think about it."

But during the next few days as they were discussing the possibilities, the rumor was passed to Ephraim that the remaining young men of Boyerker would be conscripted in the following week. The decision had been made for them.

During one of the Ukraine's worst winters, Eliezer set out on foot for Amsterdam, the precious passage money hidden in his belt. Walking during the hours of darkness, he searched out friendly peasant farmers who might let him sleep in a haystack or barn during the day. He had to be very careful, since most Russian peasants were no different from the Russian bourgeois and wanted little or nothing to do with Jews.

In spite of the bitter cold, Eliezer pushed on with the mental image of an even colder Siberian prison camp should he be caught now. This fear of death and the hope of a new life for himself and his family gave Eliezer strength and persistence much like his ancestors before him. This uncanny ability to survive for four thousand years in spite of Pharaohs, Babylonians, Romans, Crusaders, Inquisitors, Cossacks and Czars— this same ability was carrying Eliezer through the blackness of an Eastern European winter. Nearly starving to death, he begged and "borrowed" what little food he did manage, not daring to touch the precious $33 which would be his fare to New York.

Eliezer's total assets were those $33, Baruch's address in New York, and the hope of freedom in America—the golden medineh, the golden dream and the promised land—burning in his heart.

Chapter Two
Golda's Journey

Golda stared pensively into the dense, winter fog. Yusef, in her arms, was bundled in three layers of heavy clothing. At a year and a half, he was not aware of the coming three-week journey by sea to America.

The rusted Dutch vessel docked several yards away kept sounding a blast, making the one hundred emigrants nervously waiting to board even more anxious. Years of turmoil under the Czars had played havoc with their emotions. Further weakened by the two-week train ride from Russia to Amsterdam, the spectre of the rigorous ocean voyage they now faced and the worse dread of not being able to board at all kept them in emotional turmoil.

Two large, dirty bundles, always characteristic of the Eastern European emigrant, sat at Golda's feet; on the top were some smaller bundles. These bundles and Yusef were all that Golda could take with her from the old country—all, that is, except memories.

Golda had nearly died giving birth to Yusef. In labor for three days, she was assisted by an incompetent midwife who had used darning needles which pierced Yusef's head, swelling it twice its size. There was little hope for mother or child, but God was gracious and spared them both.

However, it had taken months for Golda to gain back her strength. Weakened by the ordeal, she developed rheumatic fever. Now a year and a half later, this impending journey over the Atlantic would require all the strength she could muster.

Eliezer had arrived safely in America. Living with his brother, Baruch, they together had saved enough to be able to send for both little families. Baruch's wife, Rivka, and their son, Rachmiel, both now stood by Golda and Yusef, trying to shelter each other from the winter wind.

It had been an agonizing year and a half for both Eliezer and Golda, with great gaps between correspondence. The uncertainty of his family's welfare always gnawed at him. Turmoil in Russia had reached its peak and, as usual, the Jews were blamed. Golda had wondered if she would live long enough to see her husband again. And of course there was little Yusef—he didn't even know his father.

The distance that separated them was so vast: a two-week train ride and a three-week ocean voyage. Translated into miles, that was too demoralizing to think about!

In letters to his wife, Rivka, Baruch had filled her mind with fear.

"You will make it over the ocean only if you push and take care of just yourself and Rachmiel," he had warned. "Respect and kindness are valueless. You will all be reduced to common misery if you don't try to fight for things." Never elaborating on just what those "things" were, he left that up to Rivka's colorful and pessimistic imagination. But even she found it difficult to believe that such a journey could be any worse than life in Russia.

Impatiently enduring the long wait in the cold, they all watched the first- and second-class passengers board the ship and make their way to their heated cabins. The emigrant mothers were becoming more and more anxious about their freezing children, many of whom were now whimpering and crying and trying to wrap themselves in their mother's coats.

Single men and husbands who were leaving ahead of their wives clustered together nearby, sharing similar hopes and dreams of the new world. Pioneers all, the uncertainty and discomfort did not dim their mystical dream of freedom in a new land, where Jews would not be the scapegoat for every whim of a political lunatic.

"Baruch says it's everyone for himself," Rivka reminded Golda darkly. Six-year-old Rachmiel sat on top of their bundles, thoroughly amused at the sea gulls doing incredible tricks in the sky.

"We have to be first on board!" Rivka continued stridently. "After all, we've been here the longest. Golda, why don't they put a limit on the number of passengers in third class?

This simply isn't fair! All of these people can't fit into one room like Baruch says we'll have!"

"Rivka," Golda replied softly, "we take what the good Lord provides for us and are thankful! We don't tell Him that our accommodations are not good enough!"

"You know, Golda, if we don't make it on this ship, we have to wait here in Amsterdam for a whole week longer!"

Away from the security of the only home she had ever known, Rivka's eccentricities had been multiplying since the day they left Boyerker two weeks earlier. Turning her anxieties on Golda, she often rambled on without waiting for a reply.

"Baruch says that a lot of the husbands just forget about their wives back home. They don't want them because of their backward ways. They just don't suit their husband's fancy anymore! Can you imagine that, Golda?" her voice went on querulously.

Finally a crewman came down the gangplank and moved toward the group as the ship gave another hearty blast. The crowd of emigrants pushed forward against the fence, anticipation drowning out some annoying thoughts: What will we do in America? How will we learn the language? Will it be a pagan, atheistic country like our grandparents insist?

"Push now, Golda!" Rivka cried as the gate was opened.

Mothers grasped smaller bundles and children; young men traveling alone helped mothers who could not handle everything. The entire pitiful, weary batch of aliens was going to be herded into steerage, the section of the ship that rode beneath the water.

Rivka and Rachmiel somehow surged ahead of Golda and Yusef. Two by two the emigrants walked up the narrow gangplank, entering the final stage of their journey to the new land.

Golda glanced up at the more prestigeous, wealthy clientele on the upper decks. Those first-class passengers looked down on their bedraggled shipmates with some disdain, it appeared—apathy for sure. Perhaps they really couldn't be blamed for that. What could they know about a pogrom or a Cossack? The sum total of heartache and pain that would be holed up in the ship's steerage probably could not be measured in words.

"Golda! Over here!" Rivka called. Golda gently pressed through the crowd of emigrants in an attempt to join Rivka and Rachmiel.

Two by two the motley group poured onto the deck of the ship to wait further instructions. Representing a half-dozen European countries, their languages jumbled together in the bedlam. Yiddish—a mixture of German dialects and almost every other European language—would have to be the basis for communication among these Jews. Yiddish has always reflected the travail of the wandering Jew in exile.

Was this the Sabbath, perhaps? It had been hard to keep track of the days. If it were the Sabbath, loved ones back home in the distant shtetl would soon light the candles and usher in the holy day. They would offer a prayer for Golda and Yusef, but then whisper in negative tones that they never should have gone. Nor should her husband have gone before them, even though he was young and strong. (These relatives did not know then that Golda and Yusef had left just in time—neither her parents nor Eliezer's would survive the next pogrom and usher in another Passover the coming spring.)

Golda finally made her way to Rivka whose anxious face softened now that they were safely on board. Golda surveyed the ship's human cargo. It was difficult to keep her eyes from the upper deck; there the well-dressed passengers, caught up in a spirit of festivity, didn't seem to have a care in the world. After taking one last look at Amsterdam, they scurried back into their heated cabins, to the dance floor or to the elaborate buffet that awaited them inside.

It truly did seem like a terrible injustice to Golda. Maybe a classless society wasn't such a bad idea after all. The group of frightened Jewish men and women around Golda were no less endowed with skill, talent or intellectual capacity than the Gentiles in the upper decks. Jews had no less drive, ambition or creativity. They had no less capacity to feel, to love, to dream and hope. They got just as cold and hungry as those in the first-class cabins who would be treated to several meals a

day. The Jews were willing to work just as hard for their livelihood. But these opportunities generally were stifled for them.

So that was the very reason they were bound for America!
According to Baruch and Eliezer, America stood for equality.
Golda remembered a picture postcard she received from
Eliezer. The day it came, the whole village of Boyerker came
to Golda's house to see it! It had a photo of the Statue of Liberty on it. The words engraved on the statue had been written
by a Jewish lady, Emma Lazarus. Eliezer wrote to Golda that
Emma Lazarus had said on there something about "the huddled masses yearning to breathe free." Before Golda stood
some of those huddled masses.

"What do we do now?" Rivka asked.

"We wait, and we thank God that we've made it this far,"
Golda replied pertly.

"Your attention please!" a voice shouted out of nowhere.
Finally they located another crew member standing on a platform above the emigrants. Everyone hoped that the voice
would direct them to someplace out of the cold wind.

"You will all go through that door," the man ordered in
German and then Russian. "Then down three flights of stairs
you will come to your quarters. I am afraid that somehow we
have made an error in our count. There are far too many of you
for us to take care of properly. However, we are sure that none
wants to stay behind so we are going to accommodate you the
best we can."

There had been no error in the count. In their greed, the
steamship company actually planned to cram four times as
many people into steerage as space and conditions allowed.

"You will find three levels of tiers that will be your beds,"
he continued. "Because there are so many of you, you will
have to sleep three to a bed. Mothers, if children are in the
second or third tier, please be careful that they do not fall out.
We have no railings and the sea gets very rough at times. And
please do not ask about heat in your quarters, for there is
none."

There was a collective groan and an attempt to console one
another. Then the forboding news continued.

"We can serve only one meal a day, at noon. Do not ask for a kosher meal."

More disgruntled moans followed. It appeared that everything about this excursion was going to be offensive.

"Our journey will be approximately seventeen days. We often encounter rough weather which may slow us down some. If you are sick when the weather is bad, you must stay in your quarters because it is far too dangerous to be on deck. Again, we are sorry about the overcrowded conditions. We will try to serve you the best we can."

Most of the emigrants felt defeated before they even set sail. Slowly they edged their way toward the designated door to begin what might be a three-week period of confinement. One by one they filed down the narrow steel stairway. Even the younger children's naive exuberance was quieted as they sensed the dismay of their mothers.

"Baruch was right!" came Rivka's familiar whine. "This ship isn't fit for animals. How can they do this to us? They just want our money, that's all. But they don't give us a thing in return for it!"

"They give us our husbands and our freedom," Golda quietly reminded her. "And a future for our children! Isn't that worth something to you, Rivka?"

"If we live to see it, Golda! We may freeze to death first."

Everyone scrambled for a bed—wooden tiers jutting out from a wall with filthy, smelly mattresses. The only bed left for Golda and Yusef was a tier three levels up. Rivka and Rachmiel had grabbed the tier just below that one and would be sharing it with a Jewish lady from Berlin.

Golda surveyed the situation. She would have to lift Yusef up to the third tier and her strength was nearly gone.

"May I help you?" came a soft voice behind Golda. "My name is Nina Kamenovsky," the young girl said warmly. "It looks as if I will have to share that bed with you. Let me carry your son up for you. You look very tired."

"Oh, thank you," Golda replied gratefully. "I am Golda Leshenotsky and this is my son, Yusef. I am going to join my husband, Eliezer, in New York."

Golda laboriously climbed a crude ladder to the third tier about ten feet above the floor.

"Where are you from, Golda?" Nina asked as she handed Yusef up to her.

"From Boyerker, outside of Kiev."

"I know it well!" Nina exclaimed. "I was a student at the university in Kiev. I was one of the last Jewish students allowed in there. But all of us were forced out this year. Then they drafted all the men and sent us women home. Except there was nothing for me to go home to. My village was in shambles when I got there. My whole family had been killed and the survivors fled. I guess some made it to America and Palestine."

"I am sorry about your family," Golda said as Nina finished her climb up the awkward ladder. "My husband walked on foot for weeks to escape the army. In the middle of winter he walked all night and slept in haystacks by day. He is a determined man."

"And now he has sent for you and your son," Nina concluded. "You are a fortunate woman. Not only is your man hearty—he is also in love with you and has not fallen for some fashionable American woman!"

"You see, what did I tell you!" Rivka's voice rasped from the tier beneath them. She had overheard Nina's comment.

"It's just like Baruch says!" she reminded Golda.

Golda and her new friend Nina sat on the edge of their bed and surveyed the situation, Yusef in Golda's lap. She cringed as everything she looked at and touched had a sticky layer of filth on it. There were two tiny dirty washrooms for the one hundred passengers. On a wall not far from Golda were three basins that probably had never been cleaned. These basins were to serve as dishpans, laundry tubs, baths and receptacle for those suffering from seasickness.

Suddenly the ship's engine shuddered and then settled into a steady rumble. All of the ship's machinery was just a few yards away from the steerage compartment, separated by only a thin wall. The drone of the engine would not stop day or night for three weeks. Sleep was going to be nearly impossible even if the living conditions were not so wretched.

"Baruch was right!" Rivka said as she pounded on the tier above her. "These people are robbers!"

Golda didn't answer, wondering how many more times in the next seventeen days she would hear that Baruch was right about something!

The one dim light bulb swung from its cords in the center of the room as the ship, loosed from its moorings, began the long journey. Faces were only indistinct images in the shadows moving like long fingers around the crowded room. Coughs and cries from the cold and hungry children mingled with sniffs and sighs from adults who were lonely and frightened at the prospect of life away from the shtetl. Most of the emigrants were nearly paralyzed with uncertainty. The question overwhelmed them: Had they done the right thing?

No meal was served that day. Golda had wrapped some dark brown bread for the voyage, hoping it would last for two or three days. The ship did provide hot water; many made tea or poured a little brandy into it. Some shared a bite of fruit they had brought along. Ever so slowly the incarcerated emigrants began to reach out to one another even though conversation was difficult over the engine roar.

But in less than two days, exhaustion and the miserable conditions had thoroughly demoralized everyone. It was clear that this part of the exodus would be no less of an ordeal than the situations left behind! The stormy Atlantic heaved the ship to and fro like a cheap toy. Dishes crashed into a dozen pieces on the floor. Terrified children were thrown from their beds. Even the engine roar could not drown out the cries of the children or the helpless wails of their mothers.

Seasickness was rampant. Useless to try and make it to the washroom or the basin after a while, they vomited in their beds, onto the floor or onto the bed below them. Some of the stronger men were able to make it up on deck to escape the hell of steerage. There they collapsed until the crew carried them back down to the quarters.

Lying on their bed in a stupor, all tried to block out the unending pounding of the engine and the dozen or so unblending odors that lay heavy in the air like a smothering blanket. The blare of the ship's foghorn further convinced the poor emigrants that they would never live to see the coastline of America! Their fate would be sealed forever in this floating coffin, that at any moment could ram another ship in the fog.

Too weak and sick to move, many reflected back to the old country. It was too late now, but maybe their elders had been right about this insane venture.

Golda agonized on her bed. Though she had tried to protect him, Yusef had fallen twice from the third tier; the second time he had fallen on his head. He cried for hours and Golda was sure he was seriously hurt.

This ordeal was clearly not for children. Cold, hunger and fright would leave permanent marks on those who could remember.

Rivka and Rachmiel were so sick beneath Golda that, wonder of wonders, Rivka's complaining stopped for three whole days—the only bright spot in the early stages of the journey.

Losing track of hour or day, since most hadn't seen daylight after boarding, time dragged on into one endless black night. At one point each day, however, a crew member brought down a kettle each of hot water and hot food. However, that which was contained in the food kettle was not fit for any living creature!

"The pigs at home eat better than we do!" a voice complained as a crew member brought down the day's only meal.

"You serve us the garbage from the first-class meals upstairs!" came another disgruntled comment.

"You are a bunch of crooks!" another cried. "You take our money and make us slowly starve to death!"

The kettle sat neglected on a table and sloshed and spilled on the floor until it was retrieved and replaced with another the next day.

Two days later the pounding of the waves became more intense and the blast of the foghorn more frequent. An excited crew member flew down the stairs to the steerage compartment.

"Everyone up on deck!" he cried. "We've sprung a leak! Upstairs, quick!"

Terrified screams followed. Those too weak to move suddenly had to! The ship swayed so violently that the emigrants could hardly stand. Some were helplessly tossed about, only to crash into one another and lie on the stinking floor. And then water began to gush into steerage as crew men attempted to aid the floundering people.

"I will take Yusef." Nina offered as Golda climbed down from their bed. Nina, young and strong, was a bit more adventuresome than most women.

"We are finished!" Rivka cried as she sloshed through water now two feet deep. Belongings floated about in the rapidly rising water.

Rivka pushed Rachmiel up the stairs, Golda following. Nina carried Yusef on her shoulders as he cried out in confusion and fear.

Some tried to rescue belongings and bundles but it was no use. Besides, all hands had to be free to hold onto one another or an immovable object. Anything not tied down was floating or flying precariously through the air.

"What have we done that God should drown us all in the Atlantic?" Rivka called back to Golda as they wound up the stairs.

"Please, someone carry my child for me!" came an anonymous request. "I am too weak!"

Golda's heart went out to the faceless voice. Couldn't someone help her? It required so much effort just to care for oneself.

The moment they arrived on the deck they were pounded by rain, wind and water washing over the deck. The ship's crew raced about in a desperate attempt to conquer nature. Hurling commands at one another in Dutch, they cursed each other and the storm.

One by one the emigrants filed out of their tomb and huddled together in one mass of human despair. But within seconds they were thrown to the deck and drenched in the water that heaved itself over the side railings. Some tried to pray amidst the terror of the black night; most, however, were frightened into terrified silence, except for the children whose collective cries sounded almost like a choir.

Golda, usually the last to lose hope in most any situation, had always possessed a coveted inner assurance that God was on her side in spite of any circumstances. God had demonstrated His blessing to her so many times, saving her in childbirth, from the pogroms and from early widowhood. And He had stretched Eliezer's wages so he could bring his family to America.

But a recurring thought began to menace her: perhaps God's hand of blessing was now removed from her life. It seemed, however, that it was unlike the character of God to have preserved Golda and Yusef through the ordeals of Russia only to drown them in the sea. He *must* have a higher purpose and would bring them safely to America! If so, would He answer just one more prayer of hers and spare her and little Yusef?

Dark hours passed on the deck of the ship. It did no good to wrap Yusef in her drenched coat as she felt him shivering from the cold.

Golda wondered how the first- and second-class passengers were faring. Their comforts had no doubt been interrupted. Could they gain a better understanding of the misery below?

"Papa was right," Rivka repeated over and over again like a litany through the night. "Papa was right about leaving Boyerker."

A strange hush eventually settled over everyone, even the small ones. Was it quiet resignation or was it that inner assurance that Golda sensed? Almost a holy hush?

"If I could see in the dark," Golda said softly to Rivka near by, "I think I would see a giant hand coming down out of heaven. I think that heavenly arms are enveloping us now. And I think these arms will calm the sea."

"You've always been a dreamer!" Rivka replied skeptically. "You are never realistic!"

"Golda is right." Nina agreed. "Our doubt displeases God! Our faith in His ability to deliver our people will save us. Did you hear me?" Nina said more loudly. "Everyone, listen! We must send our collective prayers to God right now! He wants to deliver us from the sea as He did from the wilderness!"

Everyone peered through the blackness to see who this self-proclaimed Moses was. And a woman at that! Nina's voice was strangely masterful.

"Everyone pray right now," Nina continued. "God will be moved to answer one hundred collective prayers. But *no one* doubt! Did you hear me? None of us can doubt Him right now!"

"Rivka, that means you, too!" Golda said, poking Rivka with an elbow.

"This must be a united effort," Nina said firmly. "If we are united in our faith, God will favor us with life."

Somehow Nina's words were heard above the foghorn and above the frantic commotion of the crew members. She spoke with uncanny authority. Even those who had given up hope united together to pray. Passionate prayer, pious prayer, mechanical prayers were heard—but all were *sincere* prayers. To the best of each one's ability, nearly one hundred united prayers ascended towards God. Some were selfish, praying only for one's own life. Others were generous prayers for the whole ship with all of its human cargo. Loud prayers in two or three languages blended heavenward.

Nothing happened immediately, to everyone's bitter disappointment! Instead, the crew began to lower several life rafts. Frequently cursing the sea, the pious emigrants and God, they muttered to one another in negative tones.

But suddenly the violent wind settled as if someone had closed a door that had let in a draft. The rain became a light drizzle and the ship stopped its heaving. An eerie silence settled over even the crew. Was this the eye of the storm, or had God answered the prayers? Skeptical crew members waited for several moments, still prepared to send everyone into the rafts. The religious ones kept praying and the doubters sat in amazement that perhaps they had had a part in this sudden change!

A faint glimmer of dawn was seen through the thick

clouds. No one moved for many minutes. Then came the command to raise the life rafts and bail out the water from the steerage. The leak had been fixed and the rain slowed to a trickle!

It was a modern-day miracle—a twentieth-century manifestation of God's continued favor toward the Jews, perhaps! Even the doubters and agnostics sat in awe of the situation and the obvious hand of God.

After the steerage was bailed out and some semblance of order was restored, Golda drifted off to sleep next to Yusef and Nina. Though they lay in soaked clothing, the one advantage to being on the third tier was that it had remained dry! Their already smelly mattress would not worsen from the dampness in their quarters.

Golda was awakened by Yusef's heavy breathing and coughing. He shifted restlessly between Nina and herself, and Golda was sure he had a fever. And every change of clothes she had was just as wet as another.

"Rivka! Nina!" Golda asked, "do either of you have any dry clothes for Yusef? He is sick!"

"Nothing, Golda," Nina answered sadly.

"Nor I," Rivka chimed in. "Everything is soaked."

"Please, someone!" Golda called into the night. "Does anyone have some dry clothes for my son? He is very sick. Can someone help me?"

There was a stirring and then a dozen or more negative replies. Everyone's belongings had been under water for hours during the storm.

"I'll get the crew," Nina said as she climbed down from the bed. "They will have something dry for him!"

The wearied emigrants seemed to emerge from their stupor. Jewish mothers would *never* stand back and watch one of their own children suffer! Nameless faces and voices called out a dozen remedies for Yusef.

"Give him something hot to drink!"

"What are his symptoms?"

"Fever, I think," Golda replied, "and chills and a cough."

"It sounds like pneumonia," came another anonymous

voice. "We must get the crew to take him upstairs where it is warm!"

"I have some castor oil!" volunteered someone else. "It cures most anything."

"Yes! I have some medicine, too," another offered. "It is supposed to be good for a dozen ailments. Would you like to try some on your son?"

"You must make the boy eat! Even that ungodly, unkosher soup they serve us. You must force him to eat!"

"Yes!" another called out. "God will understand!"

Golda waited nervously for help from the crew. Finally Nina and a crew member came down the stairs carrying a change of clothing and two heavy blankets.

Now all the mothers began to cry out, "Please, my son needs dry clothing, too! And warm blankets!"

"Help us! We are *all* soaked down here. Could we all have dry blankets?"

"Please, have mercy on us!"

"May I take my son to a warmer place on the ship?" Golda begged the crew man. "He is very sick. Listen to his breathing. I think he has pneumonia. Please, sir, have mercy on this little boy. He's not even two years old."

"I'm sorry," he replied as he handed the clothing and blankets up to Golda. "All will insist on it then. You heard them even now! We just can't make any exceptions."

"He is right," Nina agreed as she climbed back up to the third tier. "Steerage passengers have nearly mutinied on other voyages, just because one person gets special favors. Let us leave Yusef's health in God's hands and not depend on the hands of anyone on this ship."

Her mother heart in anguish, Golda pulled off Yusef's wet clothes and wrapped him in both blankets. Every hour or so, another mother would call out for a progress report on Yusef.

"Has his fever broken yet?"

"Has he been able to eat?"

"Are you sure you wouldn't like to try this medicine I have?"

The swaying of the ship had eased so that some of the

steerage passengers could go on deck during daylight hours. They gladly took the cold Atlantic air to the smelly, crowded pit below. On deck a few buried their faces in Russian and English dictionaries, trying to learn some basic words and phrases. Others played cards, visited, or played on instruments that had survived the storm and the dampness. The devout prayed several times a day. And many shared stories of the old country. As the sea calmed, so did the seasickness.

But Golda continued to agonize over Yusef. He was their first-born, Eliezer's and hers, and not yet even *seen* by his father! Days dragged on as Yusef continued to breathe heavily and have fitful coughing spells.

Golda herself was so weakened by the ordeal at sea that she seldom moved from her bed. One long day followed another without beginning or ending in the blackness of steerage. The dark brown bread had been finished days ago. Hunger pangs had finally forced many to dip into the kettle of watery soup that the crew brought down daily.

Just when Golda was ready to despair, Yusef suddenly seemed to revive himself and even sat up for a while. When that happened, the steerage compartment nearly took on a holiday mood! Then Nina walked him around and bounced him on her knee. But eventually Yusef became glassy-eyed again and his breathing became heavy. Taking a turn for the worse, he drifted back into a fitful sleep.

But one day the darkness and the boredom of steerage was interrupted as a crew member hurried down the stairs. Scurrying could be heard on deck, along with excited voices. This time they held no panic as there had been the night of the storm.

"America is in sight!" the crewman announced. "You may come up and see if you like."

Pandemonium erupted! There were instantaneous handshakes and hugs!

"Mazel tov!" (Congratulations!) everyone cried as they slapped one another on the back and kissed the little children.

Stoic, rigid men wept for joy. The infirmed seemed to be instantly drawn back into health. The irreligious even thanked God. Humorless ones cracked jokes. And the religious men, who had tried to hold everyone's faith together, put on their prayer shawls and swayed reverently and thankfully.

Pushing onto the deck, everyone squinted into the early morning haze. The seventeen-day voyage was nearing its end. But to the emigrants, this was not merely the end of a journey by sea—a way of life was coming to a close, a way of life that had included persecution, humiliation and terror. Now history for these fortunate ones, for these whom God had sovereignly spared, the nightmare was over. Ahead lay difficulty for sure; but, more importantly, the future held opportunity, free enterprise and religious freedom. Someday, maybe even prosperity for those who were willing to work hard for it!

The morning sun peeked through the clouds, dawning not only on a new day but on a whole new life!

Chapter Three

Give Me Your Tired, Your Poor—and Your Healthy

Golda was at the point of physical and emotional collapse. She held Yusef in her arms and tried to keep him from coughing. She couldn't entertain even briefly the idea of returning to Russia. Neither she nor Yusef had the strength to endure that.

After the ferry boat had brought the emigrants to Ellis Island in the New York harbor, U.S. government officials lined them up outside the main building and interrogated them. Some were marked with colored chalk on their coat lapels. Quickly it was deduced that the various colors of chalk indicated certain illnesses. America wanted only those who were healthy. Not welcome were those who probably would not be able to work and would likely end up on the charity rolls.

Nina stood on one side of Golda; Rivka and Rachmiel, on the other. Tension heavy in the air made conversation too much of a burden. All eyes were fixed on the individuals currently being questioned and marked with chalk.

These "huddled masses" were a pathetic sight. Because of the ordeal by sea, the emotional and physical trauma, they were in no condition to answer the questions that were fired at them in several languages. The procedures were tedious and time-consuming as officials made their way down the line, every so often marking a lapel with a red chalk mark, which meant suspicion of mental instability, or a "T," which meant possible tuberculosis, the "Jewish disease."

The officials of Ellis Island, overworked and short of patience, had acquired a somewhat deadened response to this off-repeated sight. Probably a defense mechanism, they had forced themselves to become calloused to the anguish and despair witnessed each day.

Some of the bone-weary emigrants were marked and then made to wait further, while others were sent inside. Occasionally a child was sent inside but the mother was made to wait outdoors for more inspection. Or worse, a child had to wait while the mother was sent into the building. Through those large double doors, one was a long step closer to the golden dream.

"Your name and your son's name," the official demanded of Golda in broken Russian. (Golda would have smiled if she hadn't been so nervous.)

"Golda Leshenotsky. This is Yusef Ahren," she answered. He would have been known as Joseph Aaron in English.

"Where are you from?"

"From a village outside of Kiev, Boyerker," Golda's voice trembled.

"When were you born?"

How should Golda communicate this in American months? The Hebrew calendar began in September or early October and lasted for thirteen months!

"Well," she began, diffident, "I don't kow how to tell you, sir, because—"

The official impatiently interrupted Golda's labored and most-likely lengthy explanation, "Who will meet you here at Ellis Island?" He still hadn't really looked at Golda, busy marking his little checks in the various boxes on the immigration forms.

"My husband will meet us here, I am sure."

"His name?"

"Eliezer Leshenotsky."

"Who paid for your ticket to America?"

"My husband paid our fares, sir." Maybe if this inspector never looked up, he wouldn't notice how ill Yusef was.

"Can you read and write?"

"Yes, sir. Russian and Yiddish."

"Not English?"

"Well, I will learn that, too!"

"How is your husband employed?"

"He sells fruits and vegetables in Manhattan."

"Does your husband earn an adequate wage or do you also plan to work in America?"

"I don't know yet, sir," Golda's voice quavered.

Suddenly poor Yusef had a coughing spell, almost right into the man's face. Obviously irritated, the official quickly glanced up. "Your son is sick," he said, but not sharply. "What is it he has?"

Golda's body stiffened in fright. They were so near and yet so far! "It's nothing—a cold perhaps." She tried to speak calmly. "It was a terrible trip over, sir. We've all been soaked for days, maybe weeks. We all lost track of the time."

Placing his pencil into a clipboard and setting it on the ground, the official took Yusef into his arms and looked at him carefully. Yusef whimpered and reached back to Golda.

"Has anyone in your family ever had tuberculosis?" he queried.

"Oh, no, sir!" And inside her silent plea, "Please, God, let him believe me!"

He put Yusef down on the ground to see if he could walk. Some immigrant children could not, and the government hesitated to take them into the country. Golda was wondering why this whole procedure hadn't been handled back in Amsterdam. Should they now be refused entrance, they could have saved themselves the terrible ordeal at sea and the crushing disappointment of having to return to Russia.

Yusef took three steps while the official held his hand. Seeming to be satisfied, the man returned Yusef to Golda.

"He is not deaf or dumb, is he?" But his voice was now more gentle than the question.

"No, sir."

"All right then, move on through that door." Golda's heart leaped in relief and excitement. The official continued, "We will want to further examine you for venereal disease, leprosy and trachoma. Your baggage will be brought inside later at the end of your inspection, which could take all day. We processed ten thousand of you people yesterday," he added warily, but he was now looking at Golda as if she were a real person, not just a check mark on a paper.

More than sixteen million immigrants, en route to America, paused at Ellis Island, aptly called the "Isle of Tears" by many whose families were torn apart there. For many reasons the most common one being sickness, one or more family members could be detained on the island and eventually sent back to the homeland. Parents agonized over the dilemma: they could either abandon their sick child or try to scrape up enough money to accompany the child back to the old country.

But for many others Ellis Island was the "Golden Door." As many as 11,000 steerage (third-class) passengers a day were "processed" in its thirty-two connected buildings. (It was only the third-class passengers who were examined there; first and second class were interviewed on the ships and then taken directly to the mainland.) The pilgrims had their Plymouth Rock; the immigrants had Ellis Island.

Golda asked the official who was motioning her toward the door into the building, "Could I not wait for my friends here?" Pointing to Rivka and Nina. "I'm afraid we will get separated and—"

"No! Move along inside now. Hurry. Hurry up!" he barked. Why did things move so slowly on Ellis Island when the immigrants were constantly being told to "Hurry up" and "Move on to the next line quickly"?

Over the years more than three thousand immigrants committed suicide on the island. Weakened beyond repair from the journey by sea, their despondency became overwhelming at the prospect of a loved one forced to turn back. Hundreds of others, unable to face return to a land of bitter oppression, tried to swim to the mainland but were caught in the currents and perished.

Entering America seemed to be more difficult than entering heaven on that Great Judgment Day! But at least the official hadn't marked Golda or Yusef with that mysterious chalk! They must have passed phase one of the entrance examination.

The first warm air they had felt in three weeks hit Golda and Yusef as they entered the immigration building. Savoring the warmth for several moments, Golda looked around at the flurry of activity in the huge room. A dozen different languages, given the common denominator of caution, apprehension and excitement, were magnified in the din of the massive hall. And here, Golda quickly saw, were more long lines.

Many of the immigrants were now painted into that proverbial corner. Should they lie about some things? In certain countries, one was able to get by officials with a bribe; in America that might bring down wrath against them or relatives already living in America. And they were often caught in a sticky web regarding employment: immigrants were more likely to be admitted if they already had a job; on the other hand, a new law prohibited certain kinds of laborers from entering.

So access into America clearly was based on God's will, fate, luck, good timing, the mood of the officials or a half-dozen other reasons—all very elusive and vague.

Golda anxiously scanned the building for Eliezer. He had received only an approximate date for the ship's arrival. Perhaps he would come that evening after work. Or maybe something had happened to him since their last piece of correspondence weeks earlier.

"Through that door!" came the shouted command in English. Though the words were meaningless to Golda, she did understand the pointing finger. Here children were being examined for trachoma, a serious eye disease that often appeared among immigrant children. Golda observed with chagrin the other unnerving examination procedures—poking, punching, and peering in personal areas done right there in the open in front of hundreds of spectators. More were being marked with chalk, questioned and sent through other mysterious doors.

Standing in line again, Golda set Yusef down to rest her arms a moment. Hanging tightly onto her skirt for security, Yusef watched carefully, intrigued by all the new sights and sounds: telephones, heaters blasting out warm air, typewriters, impatient officials speaking this strange new language. And everyone moved around so quickly, unlike Boyerker where one moved fast only if the Cossacks were coming.

"Golda! Golda!" two familiar voices called in unison from a line several yards away. There Rivka and Nina were waving to her. "Have you seen Baruch or Eliezer?" Rivka called out above the noise. Golda shook her head, and then a surge of people blocked the view. She was so glad to see that they also had made it safely inside. Their familiar faces were such a comfort amidst this sea of newness.

Golda finally stood before another Ellis Island official who was checking off more boxes on government forms. "Do you have more than one husband?" he asked.

"Oh my, no, sir!" How absurd, Golda thought.

"Do you have any money with you?" he continued.

"I had only enough for the train and the boat fare." Did America want any remaining money for an entry fee, perhaps?

"Were you ever in prison?" These mechanical questions were getting more ridiculous by the moment.

"No, sir, and neither has my husband, Eliezer."

More questions followed about her political persuasions. Was she supportive of the democratic way of life? Was she or Eliezer a part of any left-leaning anti-American movement?

Then into another line for more medical inspections. This time, however, Golda stood before a kind-looking American dressed in a white jacket. Gently lifting Yusef onto a table, he listened to his heavy breathing through a stethoscope and spoke to them both softly. Here was someone who seemed to have real compassion and concern for her situation. Relaxing a little, she felt that somehow her hope for a future in America rested on this one individual.

"You have had a hard trip, haven't you?" he asked, not taking his eyes off Yusef. Golda breathed a sigh of relief when he skipped the dreaded eye exam. Earlier she had seen other children enduring its agonies.

"Yes," she answered him, "my son became very wet and cold when the ship was in a storm. I think he is finally getting over a cold," she went on hopefully.

"We have an infirmary here at Ellis Island," he said. "I could keep you both here for a week or so, but I think your son has pneumonia. I want you to take him directly to Mt. Sinai Hospital. Who is here to meet you?"

"My husband will be here eventually. He may be here now. I've been behind these doors for hours. He would have no way of knowing where I am."

The doctor called to someone in English. "Help this woman find her husband," he commanded. "Then see to it that they are taken directly to Mt. Sinai Hospital, even if you have to take them there yourself. And carry the boy for her—this woman is exhausted from the journey."

Oh, America was a land of hope and promise after all! "Thank you, sir!" Golda murmured gratefully. "And may God bless you! My friends are over there. May I tell them where I am going?"

"Of course. And don't forget to pick up your bundles before you leave the building. They are being kept for you in the baggage area until you have passed all the entrance regulations. Give this slip of paper to one of the officials in the outer area. It says that you and your son may now go on to the mainland, that you have met our entrance requirements and plan on applying for American citizenship. Welcome to our country."

"Welcome to our country!" What wonderful words those were! Golda wished she could sing them aloud over and over again.

Golda hugged Nina and Rivka. "Yusef and I passed," she cried. "We made it! But now I must take Yusef to a hospital because they think he has pneumonia. Rivka, if I see Baruch out there, I will try to send him to you. Nina, what will you do now? Where are you going from here?"

"I have an address," she replied. "I have friends here from Kiev who are expecting me, Golda. But we will meet again, I am sure!"

Kissing them all good-bye, Golda followed the handsome young American and Yusef to the outer area. Pulsating with anxious, impatient cries and movement, the crowd of friends and relatives strained for a glimpse of a familiar face.

Golda finally spotted Eliezer. He looked so different, so American! And his beard was shaved off! But Golda's heart leaped for joy and her face lit up like a light. "Eliezer! Eliezer!" she cried. "Over here!"

Pushing through the crowd and stumbling over baggage, they finally reached one another. The agonizing journey was over; someone was here to take care of her and Yusef. Their pounding hearts beat as one as Golda laid her head on Eliezer's chest.

Golda choked back her tears of joy as she introduced Yusef to his father. Eliezer's eyes were full, too, as Yusef's little arms circled his neck. They were a family again!

Golda knew that some of her friends felt her to be an impractical dreamer. She did realize, though, that there would be hard times ahead still, with many frustrations and disappointments. But now God had spared them from the Cossacks, from conscription, from the perils of the sea, and He had spared Yusef from almost certain death. Surely God's goodness to the Leshenotsky family would extend into their life in this new land!

Chapter Four

Christ-Killer!

The Lower East Side had become the most densely popu-
lated area in New York. By the time Golda and Joseph arrived, it was nearly bursting at the seams with more than a
half million Jews. The whole character of New York was
changing. Orthodox Jews paraded in their unique dress. Yiddish became the second language in New York. And yet in
spite of the overcrowded conditions, the filth, the exhaustion
and the desperately low wages, the Jews had the second lowest
rate of return to the old country.

But without question, it was back to ghetto life again. In
Russia it would have been called a shtetl. To some it must
have seemed like a treadmill with a Jewish ghetto at the beginning and the end. The setting was different now, of course.
The shtetls didn't harbor squalid tenements, saloons, putrid
poolrooms, garbage in the streets and sinister red lights in
windows. Nor did they have row after row of brick tenements—perhaps twenty to a block—with children dangling
precariously out of the windows. Or the sight of clean but
ragged laundry drying on dirty fire escapes.

Life would still not be easy for the "hordes of Jewish
aliens," as they were called. They were easily distinguished as
they made their way to the Lower East Side of New York.
Awkward, unkempt and timid, they were always carrying
their bundles, looking for an address on a ragged letter. Someone—a relative or a friend, or even a stranger who had survived the journey some years earlier—would take them in until they could get their feet on the ground.

The confusion, loneliness and weariness—and perhaps the
first few weeks or months with strangers—all added to the
pain of adapting to this new land and its strange ways. Many

found it difficult to adjust to units of time that strictly divided a day. Why, the sun comes up and goes down as regular as these fancy American clocks, doesn't it?

Eliezer had found a small fifth-floor "walk up" for his family. At the back end of the brownstone were two cramped little rooms: the kitchen/sitting room/dining room in one and an even smaller bedroom for the other. They shared a bath down the hall with the other families on the floor.

Golda's first consternation at the sight of the dirty little rooms and the depressing backyard view from the windows quickly gave way to her usual optimism and determination. Under her capable supervision, even Eliezer (he had felt totally helpless when facing those two rooms alone) was able to help turn them into a cozy home.

Golda's most prized possession, a small but gleaming samovar, had survived the ocean voyage in one of her bundles. She and Eliezer both had a lump in their throats as they looked at it sitting on the scarred, second-hand table and remembered it so proudly shining on the handmade table in their little house in Boyerker. But the warm memories were demolished by the terrifying ones—the horses thundering by, the shattered glass, the shrill cries and screams.

"Oh, Eliezer," Golda whispered as she slipped her arms through his, "we'll have a new life here in America! We'll make it work." Eliezer nodded wordlessly.

Thousands of Jewish immigrants spent sixty hours a week in the various "sweatshops" of New York City. Eventually 90% of the garment industry was in Jewish hands. Too tired to fight for anything better than standing over a hot iron or bent over a sewing machine, they ended their days in such a manner. At least they had escaped the Czars and now they had religious freedom. Maybe their sons and daughters could have a chance for a better life. Education was the ladder that could elevate their children to where they could see beyond the tenements of the Lower East Side.

Eliezer could not support his family on his $5 a week he now earned as a laborer. He was able to get a job as a ticket puncher with the subway system and earned $10 a week. But when Joseph was three, a daughter, Leah, joined the family. Somehow Eliezer had to launch out on his own to make a living wage for them.

A rumor flourished in the Lower East Side that all American millionaires had begun as peddlers! With a pack on their back the hopeful climbed tenement stairs all day long. Having no particular skills (at least ones that would fit in a big city), they realized the only alternative to peddling was to work in the sweatshops from early morning to late at night.

Peddlers merchandised everything from fish to hardware. Some carried as much as 120 pounds of goods on their shoulders. Those who could afford it rented a horse and wagon.

The peddlers held no great honor. Signs appeared: "No peddlers or beggars allowed." Doors were slammed in their faces all day long and children taunted them. Every now and then a spool of thread, or an apple, or some potatoes, or a can opener was sold. The only way they could have some dignity restored would be to have a regular route and customers. They dreamed of saving their profits—pennies at first—and establishing their own business. Many succeeded at that ambition; countless more were eventually wiped out in various economic depressions.

And so for Eliezer it was back to peddling, this time on his own. For $2 a day he rented a horse and for $1 a day a wagon, filling it with produce from the Farmer's Market. If he could sell his wagon full of fruits and vegetables in one day, he could make an adequate profit to support his family. And he was able to be outdoors and had a certain degree of freedom to roam as he wished. He was still a country boy at heart who longed for the simple life-style of the shtetl.

Joining the host of peddlers that circulated the Lower and Upper East Side, Eliezer called out his wares as he rode along. Shop owners were furious; they had to pay sizable rents for their buildings. Peddlers were free to roam without such expenses.

"Mr. Rabinovitz!" Eliezer called out as he climbed down from the wagon. "I have some grapes today that you and your family will love! You can get them just in time for Shabbat. They are only a nickle a bunch."

"I'll give you three cents, Leshenotsky, and not a penny more!"

"Rabinovitz! I have a family to support! I *must* have a nickle."

"Three cents, Leshenotsky. Take it or leave it!"

"America goniff!" (American thief) Eliezer cried out a dozen times a day, at least inside. America was too dog-eat-dog for him, too rigid and structured. Everything revolved around money.

To avoid such haggling, Eliezer finally changed his route and stayed in the Gentile neighborhoods. His ruggedly handsome face looked more Irish than Jewish, so he was generally well received in those areas. He made twice as much money there, for the Gentiles didn't bargain over every item; but he and his family had to give up the Sabbath, for Saturday was his busiest day.

The Jewish Sabbath was particularly important to these "displaced persons." It was especially welcomed after a sixty-hour work week for many men. It also was a time to be with the family, or to kibbutz in the synagogue. Jews around the world could stop and remember that they were Jews, no matter what that fact cost them. The Jewish man may be a lowly sweatshop worker six days a week, but he is restored to his true character as a prince of God one day a week, beginning at sunset on Friday night. The Sabbath is a covenant between God and Israel.* On the Sabbath the Jew acknowledges God's ownership of the world.

The lack of this observance was no small loss to the Leshenotsky home. Religious traditions and worship were the cohesive force that had held families close together over the centuries. In fact, denying it would deprive children of their Jewishness in an irreparable way.

After several months of hard work, Eliezer finally was able to buy his own horse! Wild horses were frequently brought to a stable on the edge of town. Surrounding the stable was a corral where the horses were broken in, sometimes taking days of work. Eliezer selected one, gently put the harness around it

*Exodus 13:12-17.

and slipped the bit in its mouth. While the horse snorted nervously, Eliezer harnessed it to the wagon. He climbed on the wagon, snapped the whip next to the horse's ear, then held onto the reins for dear life! He let the horse kick, buck and race for a full fifteen minutes. The wagon twisted and turned and banged over the cobblestones; but Eliezer was the master of the contest!

The next day the procedure was repeated and this time the horse kicked less furiously. Within a week the horse was not just broken—it had become totally dedicated, submissive and obedient to Eliezer! He repaid that dedication. Each Sunday, Eliezer's day off, he would clean and brush the horse and check its shoes to make sure none were loose. The horse was well fed, and Eliezer paid $5 a month to keep it in a stable.

Their relationship became a classic study in loyalty and devotion. The horse learned Eliezer's route; the reins lay in his lap and were used only to direct it away from danger. His horse knew every turn and angle. It knew it should go slowly down hills and steadily up them. It knew when the work day should be coming to a close. If Eliezer was on his route too long, the horse would turn his head to the side and try to look back at him—a gentle reminder to his master that it was time to end the day.

If Eliezer stayed in a tenement building too long delivering goods, his horse walked up to the door of the building, as if he wanted to enter it if necessary and retrieve him. If Eliezer had to make a special delivery away from the usual route, the horse became confused and disoriented.

On Sundays, Nathan's Barber Shop was the rallying spot for the men on the Leshenotsky's block. Sunday was everyone's day off, and the men automatically planned to spend half a day there away from the wife and children.

Eliezer, like all the men, climbed into Nathan's chair expecting the V.I.P treatment as well as a rousing conversation. The man in Nathan's chair was temporarily king. He received Nathan's undivided attention—hot towels, shave, haircut. All the men knew that this was their little corner of the world—more so than the synagogue perhaps. Here they had frank man-talk and escaped the nervous wives and noisy children. They could count on leaving physically refreshed and satisfied with meaningful dialogue. If one hadn't arrived by 9:00 a.m., there was an automatic four-hour wait. But nobody complained.

It was a paradoxical world into which little Joseph was initiated. It was a world of tragedy and triumph, pathos and excitement, bitter disappointment and crazy Jewish humor. A world that longed for financial freedom after centuries of repression and exile. A world of doting Jewish mothers and stoic, overworked Jewish fathers. A world filled with overcrowded, miserable conditions that did not produce miserable children. A world of extreme poverty that bore few children who felt deprived. A world where quarrels were perhaps merely peaceful rituals. A world of piety and poverty still, and of spiritual pursuit which seldom filled the vacuum in the hearts of their children.

It was punctuated infrequently by joyous outbursts of celebration! Such was the case that deliriously happy night when Joseph was five. He watched from the front hall window with amusement and curiosity as his elders tore through the streets in their pajamas and underclothes, shouting, "Shalom! Shalom!" The First World War had just ended. Men grabbed garbage can lids and beat them with spoons. Carrying on half the night, dancing in the streets, hugging and kissing most anyone, men even danced with women—a custom strictly forbidden in the old country!

"Peace has come! Peace has come!" they shouted and sang.

Peace! So elusive and temporary to the Jewish heart.

Joseph entered Hebrew School that year. Twenty children of all ages sat at Rabbi Shapiro's round table. The youngest children were at his left and they received intense, personal instruction. The older children were at his right and had to wait for him to finish with the smaller children. Patiently he took his pencil and went over the Hebrew alphabet a hundred times with the young ones. As a student progressed, he would move towards a coveted chair on the far right.

But even after eight years of Hebrew School, Joseph never learned what it was he was reading in Hebrew! That was always a frustration to him. He could make the Hebrew sounds but he didn't understand the meaning. He did look forward, though, to the Rabbi's Bible stories! The Rabbi would lean back on his chair and adjust his glasses for the occasion. Even the older children sat on the edges of their chairs when Rabbi Shapiro told the story for the day. One was proud to be a Jew when it was learned what one's ancestors went through. It was easier to take when the little Gentile boys punched Joseph as he ran home from Hebrew School. Easier, too, when they called him "kike" or "Christ-killer." Joseph didn't know what that all meant, but he knew it wasn't good. Boys twice his age took delight in punching him just to let him know he was a Jew.

Then another son entered the Leshenotsky home, and, as in every ghetto family, space became the object of supreme desire. A room to oneself was a luxury beyond reach! It wasn't unusual to come home and find one's cot in the kitchen had been given away to some relative or friend just off the boat from the old country. The Leshenotsky family was fortunate in that so far they hadn't been required to share their flat with a whole family! (It was common for two families to share one cold-water, cockroach-infested tenement room.)

Because of this, the streets became home for the children. Tenements, shops, synagogues—they belonged to the adults. But the streets prepared the children for the future. Hester Street could give them an education in the evils of the world. One could explore the dangerous world of the Gentiles if he dared go beyond Cherry Street where the Irish lived, or west of the Bowery where the Italians settled.

Baseball in the streets became the badge of America for Jewish boys. A bat could be a broomstick; a ball made from tightly wound twine. It didn't matter that the narrow streets of the Lower East Side made a terrible baseball diamond. The barber shop might be first base, a manhole cover second base, the candy store third base, and an open manhole might be home plate. It was definitely a boys' world, but the girls didn't seem to mind. In fact, every day Jewish men thanked God that they were born neither Gentiles nor women! The Jewish life-style in both the old and new country pointed the girls in one direction only: marriage and homemaking.

As filthy as the streets of the Lower East Side were, the few brief years or months of freedom were cherished by the young. Jewish childhood lasted only a short time. As soon as a child was able, he would have to work after school and weekends. Some shined shoes or delivered groceries to the wealthy Gentiles. Some hauled coal or wood on foot for miles. Others, like Joseph, helped their fathers peddle.

For a boy of seven like Joseph, the first few days were an adventure! Pa might even let him hold the reins to the horse! A kid could really learn the ways of the world from a top a peddler's wagon, he thought, strolling casually from neighborhood to neighborhood. The fire engines intrigued him the most; they were pulled by the most graceful horses, snorting and speeding to some tenement fire. Pa's horse was always frightened at the commotion, but Eliezer could calm him easily. Speaking softly to the horse, Eliezer could get its nervous, shifting body to relax.

But after spending a week with Pa after school and for sixteen hours on Saturday, the novelty had worn off for Joseph. His legs were nearly ready to give out.

"Go up and see what Mrs. Murphy wants today," Eliezer commanded. "She's in apartment seven on the top floor."

Running up two steps at a time, Joseph got Mrs. Murphy's order. He ran back to Pa, who filled her request for ten pounds of potatoes. Then he tore up the stairs again to deliver the goods.

"You should be able to deliver this in less than five minutes!" Pa said.

But Joseph hadn't caught his breath from the first run up the stairs. The second time up, with ten pounds of potatoes, his legs were rubber and his heart was pounding. But since Pa could do it in less than five minutes, his son was expected to do the same.

By noon on Saturday Joseph's legs felt like lead from a

hundred runs up narrow, dirty stairways. And the workday wasn't even half over yet! Any complaint or whine would bring on Pa's displeasure.

Eventually the Gentile kids caught on to the fact that a Jewish lad was entering their domain almost every day. Only the biggest, strongest Jewish boys would dare do that! Risking ridicule, a stoning and probably a punch in the nose, the big kids could handle themselves. But now a dumb little kid had come into their neighborhood who could not defend himself! What an opportunity to take out some aggressions on him.

"Kike! Kike!" a band of four kids screamed at Joseph.

"Christ-killer!" came another cry.

Eliezer tuned them all out rather easily. To Joseph, Pa always seemed to be off in another world somewhere. He seldom communicated or reacted.

Keeping his eyes straight ahead, "Prejudiced goyim" (Gentiles), he muttered this time and shook his head.

"What's it all about, Pa?" Joseph knew he was safe as long as he was on the wagon with Eliezer.

"Pay them no mind, son. Who can understand the thinking of the Gentiles? We Jews quit trying a long time ago and now we stay to ourselves as much as possible."

At seven years of age Joseph couldn't really grasp prejudice or anti-Semitism. But he could see it and sometimes feel it.

Pa picked up the reins that had been resting in his lap and drew his horse to a stop.

"Mrs. O'Toole may need some things today, son. Run up and see what she wants."

Joseph disappeared into the brownstone tenement in the heart of the Irish ghetto. He couldn't quite understand why Pa spent his every working hour with the Gentiles when he spoke so poorly of them. Maybe they were just good customers, even though many of them were as poor as the Jews.

Moments later Joseph bounded down those same stairs only to find six Gentile boys lined up in front of the building. They all had a sneer on their faces that spelled trouble. Joseph glanced at Eliezer who was apparently going to let Joseph learn a hard lesson on his own. He cautiously made his way down the outside stairs as three boys lined up on each side of him.

"Whacha doin' here, dirty Jew?" one of the boys taunted. All were twice his size. One more pleading look at Pa confirmed the fact that Joseph was on his own.

"Leave me alone!" came the standard reply.

"We don't want you on our block," one of them yelled. "This time we'll just warn you. We're gonna let you off the hook easy. Beat it."

Joseph darted past them, but not until all six boys each took one swing at him. Nursing the wounds, he climbed back up on the wagon.

"Pa! Did you see that?" he whimpered, rubbing a wound.

"What does Mrs. O'Toole want?"

How could Pa care so little about the ordeal?

"Just some carrots, Pa. But *please* don't make me take them up to her!"

"Nonsense. That's your job." Pa dropped a bundle of carrots in a bag.

"But, Pa—"

"Joseph, if I'm to sell this wagon load today, we can't take time to think about anything but business. You and I have to provide for your ma and the other kids. Hurry up and bring these carrots to Mrs. O'Toole!"

The boys had scattered, but suddenly realized that the target of their abuse had actually returned in spite of their warning! Rallying again, they lined up outside the front steps. Because of their size and number, they all laughed and sneered with self-confidence. This kind of sport was more fun than baseball!

Joseph surveyed the situation from a hallway window. The six boys had lined up like an army regiment set for battle. At a young age, he was being forced to think for himself and to employ clever methods of self-preservation.

He turned and followed the stairway to the roof of the building. Surveying the situation from the rooftop, he saw that a space of about three feet separated the building from

52

the one next to it. In one easy jump he flew across to the other building, then came down those stairs and back onto the street from another angle. He quietly made his way to the wagon and climbed back on. As it rattled its way down the street, the boys realized they had been fooled!

"We'll get you for sure next time, kike!" they yelled. Their pride was devastated—a little Jewish boy half their age and size had outsmarted them. They wouldn't forget that.

Golda waited at home each evening, ready to mend Joseph's wounded body and heart. His sustenance—emotional as well as nutritional—always came from her. This was no different than in most other Jewish households where the mothers held families together. Outsiders might call her ministrations to his wounds folk medicine. Actually an accumulation of experience, heresay and common sense meant that doctors and hospitals were used only as a last resort.

"God bless Dr. Moskowitz! But may we never need him!" Mama often would say. If castor oil and a dozen home remedies could not solve a problem, *then* the doctor would be summoned.

Joseph knew that Mama could always be found in the kitchen—the center of activity. And now they had one whole room for the kitchen since another family had moved and the Leshenotskys had rented two more rooms for their growing family. There was a real sense of community as fathers sat at the kitchen table and read a newspaper, children did school work and a new house guest might ramble on in Yiddish about his recent voyage over from Russia.

Mother was a queen in the kitchen; it took on her very character. From early morning until late at night, she lovingly prepared meals for her family. She had to be a practical person, for she had many mouths to feed; she simply saw to it that it was done. Many a Jewish mother was worn with fatigue—heavy, shapeless and prematurely aged. But she was bound to create an oasis for her family, trying to sustain the morale of all those around her. She would mediate quarrels, soothe hurts and hold things together in this new world. Clearly the emotional center of the family, the mother was at the hub and everyone turned to her.

Having to make pennies stretch for several meals, she shopped until she found where she could get some fresh fish or vegetables for maybe a penny less. If it wasn't Passover she had to satisfy her family with inexpensive food—bread, potatoes, tea and soup meat. It would be another generation before an immigrant Jewish family could take for granted plenty of tasty food two or three times a day.

Jewish mothers longed for more comfortable, secure life, and yet how could they ask any more from husbands already working twelve or fourteen hours a day in the sweatshops or on the peddlers' carts?

"Eliezer Leshenotsky!" Golda scolded as she rubbed some smelly ointment on her son's bruises. "If you're going to make your son work with you, the least you can do is defend and protect him!"

"If I defend him now, he won't be able to take care of himself when he gets older," Eliezer replied without raising his head from the newspaper. "He might just as well learn the ways of the world while he is young. They won't get any better. Some day he will grow up and leave New York. He will face a lifetime filled with people who would like to rid the world of one more Jew. So I am doing him a favor."

That was all Pa would say. There was some truth to that. Golda could harangue all she wanted, but Eliezer would not respond further.

He was right, in fact. The ghettos of New York were good training grounds for facing a world that wasted no love on Jews.

Chapter Five
We Can't Know for Sure

Joseph and Eliezer rode nearly a mile without speaking that brisk, fall day. At age eleven, Joseph was beginning to feel that he was an adult. By now he knew that the chilly wind of fall was just a prelude to a winter of misery—misery on the peddler's wagon and misery in the tenement flat that was only occasionally heated.

By now Joseph disliked every facet of the peddling business. He could not find one redeeming virtue connected with it. Other Gentile children continued to hurl stones and verbal abuses at him. And Saturdays dragged on endlessly—a *whole day* of peddling! The business had robbed his family of a religious life, a significant part of the lives of all Jewish families, even those less religious than previous generations. And his grades were suffering because he had to join his father each day after school.

Today the wagon followed a street cleaner roaming the Lower East Side with a pail and a broom. It was not uncommon for ghetto women to wrap their garbage in newspaper and simply throw it out the window. More than once such refuse had come crashing down on the wagon. Just as often, however, it splattered on top of someone on the street below the window. Great cursings followed as the unsuspecting victim on the ground tried to figure out from which window it had been thrown! For those who watched, it provided a few brief moments of comic relief!

But then some Gentile boys got the idea of dropping other things from the rooftops of the Jewish tenements. They dropped bricks and bottles on the children as they played on the sidewalks or alleys below. In a flash they disappeared over a rooftop, impossible to catch. Numberless innocent children were injured, and soon even the adults had to stop congregating on the sidewalks beneath the rooftops.

But today Eliezer and Joseph were going to see something much worse than flying bricks or garbage. As the horse wound its way through their neighborhood on its way to the Irish ghetto, Joseph's eye caught someone on the top of a building. (His eyes were frequently fixed on the rooftops in his neighborhoods in an attempt to spot the Gentile kids up to their dirty tricks.)

The man on the rooftop stood motionless for several moments. Then without warning he jumped from the roof and fell, crushed and bloodied, not ten feet from the wagon! Joseph was stunned into a stupor. He wanted to cry or scream or run but he couldn't. Eliezer picked up the reins and hurried his horse on down the street.

"Pa, why did he do it?" he whispered in bewilderment.

"Maybe life was just too much for him. Maybe he was tired of working in a sweatshop all day. Who knows? He probably couldn't adjust to America, or he missed his family in the old country."

"Pa, what happens to him now?"

"I don't know," Eliezer answered candidly.

"Pa, what happens to a man when he dies? Where does he go?" Why hadn't Joseph considered this question before? Plenty of people died every day in the ghetto. But he never witnessed the event in this gruesome way.

"Who can say where he goes? Maybe heaven, maybe hell. And maybe just six feet under the ground. We can't know for sure."

Eliezer's words reverberated throughout Joseph's head. Having just stared death in the face, he wanted to know for sure.

"Uncle Moishe will be coming to live with us for a while," Pa went on. "He is a religious man. He just lost his wife and he would like to stay with us for a while. You may ask him those questions."

With obvious finality, Pa sank back into his own private world.

But Joseph relived the vivid death scene all day. The same questions repeated themselves in his mind up each flight of stairs: What happens after death? Where does one go from here? Is that all there is to life, that it should come to a pitiful end in a single leap from a building?

"We can't know for sure." He couldn't shake those uncertain words from his thoughts. Even at age eleven, he knew that religion—faith in a living God—had to produce some certainties. If not, why bother to go through a lot of time-consuming rituals and traditions?

Eliezer turned his horse into the Italian ghetto. Then Joseph saw with his own eyes a horse-drawn hearse headed their way! As the two passed one another, he could see a white casket showing through the window. Following the hearse were a half-dozen musicians playing a funeral dirge. Behind them followed the wailing Italian family.

This was all too much for one day! Joseph stood up in the wagon and looked back as the funeral procession wound on down the street. He listened as the mournful cries grew more faint. For the second time in one day he had to consider the subject of death! This was the point at which the question of life after death became an obsession to him. As he matured the questions grew more complicated and the answers more elusive.

School continued to be interrupted by peddling and odd jobs, but perhaps his *real* education was obtained from his pa's wagon. All was there in front of him: gangland fights, crime, violence, perversion, cruelty. Poor blacks or Puerto Ricans, whose vision could not conceive of better days, were resigned to poverty; tomorrow would be the same as today. But for the Jews, there was always a better day ahead.

Every so often a special day stood out against the fabric of life. Joseph savored that most recent memory—the day Izzy Horowitz challenged Rocky Muscone to a fist fight because Rocky had dropped some bottles on Izzy's sister. A hundred kids gathered at the vacant lot on 99th Street to watch Rocky reduce Izzy to shreds.

The Jewish kids lined up on one side of the lot and the Italian kids on the other. They carried on a verbal war for several minutes until their two representatives faced off. Izzy didn't have a chance and everyone knew it! He was a full twenty pounds lighter than Rocky. Rocky, who wanted to be a prize-fighter, worked out every day.

At the sound of a whistle the dust began to fly and Izzy and Rocky pounded one another to a pulp! A hundred kids shouted their support, and dozens of neighbors peered out of their windows to see what the commotion was all about.

But when the dust settled, it was Rocky who lay flat on his back with a bloody nose. Izzy gave him one final kick while he lay on the ground.

The Jewish kids went wild! For once the underdog had won something! For two days a carnival-like atmosphere raged throughout the neighborhood. The Jews had trounced the Italians, and for a few moments in their history, nothing else mattered! Not cold-water flats, anti-Semitism, bed bugs, or even peddling! In fact, Joseph rode on the wagon like a king for days—especially in the Italian neighborhood. He was temporarily on the winning side in the never-ending battle. The Jews would be dethroned quickly enough, but this week he was proud to be a Jew—not just because they had defeated Pharaoh and Haman but because they had defeated Rocky Muscone!

The day Uncle Moishe arrived, Joseph's cot was moved to the kitchen near a window. What little heat the building had was frequently turned off even on the coldest of days. His feet were precariously close to the window the night the temperature dipped well below zero. Landlords seldom fixed the cracks in windows and on this particular night the cold air filtering in did its work; by morning his feet were numb and discolored, obviously frozen as were the tips of his ears. Mama pushed him to the hospital in a baby cart! But the glorious verdict was that he would have to stay completely off his feet for three months! That meant three months with no peddling—the best news yet in his young life!

Few people had an influence on Joseph like Uncle Moishe. He was a devout Jew who wrapped himself in his prayer shawl and prayed most of the day. There was something mystical and strangely appealing about worshipping God. One could easily become jealous of the close relationship Uncle Moishe seemed to have with God. The spiritual hunger pains grew stronger within Joseph as he sat at home with little to do but talk to Uncle Moishe. He had been savoring his first question for Uncle Moishe for several days. He was sure that if anybody had a clue to that answer it would be Uncle Moishe. His thoughts seldom drifted from God or the Bible. But the thing that spoke the most loudly to Joseph was that Uncle Moishe had handled the death of his wife so well. The obvious conclusion was that he knew something more about death than anyone else.

"What happens to us after death, Uncle Moishe?" he finally asked.

"Well, you keep the law, Yusef," he said softly. "You do good deeds and pray all the time. You fast and pray on Yom Kippur. You just do the best you can, Yusef, and God will forgive your sins."

"But what if I slip and do something bad? What if on the last day of my life I really sin and cancel out all the good things?"

"Well, God is the judge."

"But maybe, just maybe, I can undo all the good things by one little mistake, Uncle Moishe?"

"God is just."

Uncle Moishe sensed the intensity of Joseph's need. He sat down across from him at the kitchen table and looked at him for several moments.

"Yusef, you are a serious young man. Judaism needs young men like you. Finish Hebrew School and get Bar Mitzvad and maybe you will become a Rabbi some day. It grieves me, Yusef, because our beliefs are watered down here in America. There is not the religious enthusiasm there was in the old country. Men don't go to the synagogue every day. Some work on the Sabbath. Men shave their beards and listen to sermons in English. Sometimes the women even sit with the men in the synagogues! They think more about their social programs than they do about God."

The American way of life was hardly conducive to old world traditions. It was awkward to have to pray several times a day or to have the old-world appearance, complete with uncut hair and Orthodox dress. Dietary laws were often difficult to comply with in America. Younger Jews were eager to get rid of the old values and traditions as quickly as possible. In fact, they could see few advantages to being a devout Jew.

But even now at eleven years of age, Joseph observed that Judaism seemed to be a religion of cold-faced, pharisaic and inflexible men caught up in tradition that didn't do much to alter behavior. Perhaps it was a religion to some Jews just because they were born into it. Was it really changing lives? More and more Jews born in America were raising similar questions, often driving a wedge between the generations.

"So tell me what happens to me if I sin on the last day of my life, Uncle Moishe? Do I go to heaven?"

"Well, I can't say for sure, Yusef."

There it was again! That agonizingly uncertain reply! I can't say for sure! If religion can't be a life of certainty and not doubt, what good is it?

"I'm afraid of death," Joseph admitted frankly. "I have bad dreams about it. Death seems so final and so hopeless. All I see is wailing and mourning and people without hope. I saw a man die, Uncle Moishe. He jumped from a tenement building and landed not ten feet from Pa and me. I can't forget. I relieve it every day, it seems. I want to know where he went when he died."

Uncle Moishe sat quietly and listened.

"Your peddler's wagon has matured you too quickly, Yusef. You have seen life at its worst from your vantage point. The stinking ghettos of New York have made you a man at eleven years of age. America is corrupt and evil. Every day I pray that the Mashiach (Messiah) will come and save us all while there is still the time."

"Who is He?"

"Well, we don't know, Yusef. But when He comes, the whole world will see Him and He will save our people. He will bring peace to the world forever. Who knows, maybe Elijah will announce His coming this Passover."

Joseph reflected on the Passover Seder his family had each year. A place was always set at the table for Elijah. He would come back some day and announce the return of the Messiah; each year, however, that event ended in disappointment.

Who was this Messiah anyway? Some mystery man who was created in someone's imagination? Was He an elusive pipe dream, a dream that had given his ancestors a ray of hope enabling them to endure centuries of persecution and dispersion?

"So how can the whole world see His coming at the same time?" Joseph had visions of the Messiah blowing one gigantic shofar so loudly that the world would hear it everywhere.

"It will be a miracle, I guess," Uncle Moishe replied.

"So why does He delay His coming?" he asked.

"So that you and I, Yusef, can prepare the world. We must make the world ready for Him. I think He will come in your lifetime. I think you will live to see the Messiah. But only if you and your generation firmly embraces Judaism again. That is why young men like you must grow up to be the spiritual leaders of our people. Our people, Yusef, have been given the assignment to make the world ready for Him. But instead we work on the Sabbath and we eat food that sometimes is not kosher. We delay His coming."

Something in Uncle Moishe's words rang true! He had touched that strange chord deep within Joseph that chimed every time a spiritual truth was spoken. The answers, vague and uncertain, seldom satisfied him. Monumental loopholes and gaps were left beside contradictions that were seldom explained. And then there were lives that were changed very little. Most everyone talked a big game but lived lives that varied from gross selfishness to out-and-out corruption. That is, most everyone except for Uncle Moishe. He lived what he taught and it worked in his life. There was little doubt in Joseph's mind that one could have a close relationship with God which ultimately would be reflected in one's very character. Religion and faith didn't have to be dead ritual; it had obviously strengthened Uncle Moishe.

This mysterious spiritual quest began to intensify in Joseph. He had seen it work—to some degree anyway—in one man. That shred of hope was sufficient for him to keep on with the pursuit.

Chapter Six
Elijah: Proclaimer of Messiah

Passover brought to Joseph more than the usual amount of anticipation for spring. These few occasions—Passover, Rosh Hashanah, Yom Kippur, Hanukkah—brought the family together in rigorous spiritual activity. These times lessened the ache in Joseph's heart.

The Leshenotsky home was "kosher" with separate dishes for meat and dairy products; and in further ceremony an all "new" set of dishes had to be retrieved from the top closet shelf for the Passover meal.

In Jewish homes around the world, all traces of bread are removed at Passover time. Joseph's family searched for any remaining leaven. The children had placed bread crumbs throughout the house earlier. Then Eliezer turned into a sleuth and the children followed him in an attempt to "discover" the leaven. Then, in keeping with tradition, the bread was placed in a wooden spoon, wrapped in a cloth and thrown into a small bonfire in the street.

The house, too, had been scoured, a spring cleaning to end them all! Mama cleaned the windows, walls, floors, cupboards, curtains and bedding.

Then the day of Passover was given over to personal cleanliness. The women had to take a "mikva" (total bath). Small children were bathed in kitchen sinks or tubs. The men and boys went to a Turkish bath where they sat baking, engaged in heavy conversation. They would steam, sweat and then jump into the pool.

Nails were trimmed, hair washed and clothes cleaned and pressed.

Their mouths watering in anticipation of the meal that Jewish mothers had been preparing for days, at last everyone gathered at the table for the Seder service. For once children stopped talking without having to be told to do so. The family, clean and sparkling with eyes shining in the candlelight, looked expectantly toward the head of the household.

Then the man of the family conducted the service. For these moments he was not just a peddler, an oppressed sweatshop worker, an unsuccessful breadwinner. He was the exalted head of the home and all honor was given to him.

The whole family, including Uncle Moishe, sat at perfect attention as Pa began the ceremony.

"We are about to begin the recitation of the ancient story of Israel's redemption from bondage in Egypt. The purpose of this Seder is to afford us the opportunity to recall the dramatic and miraculous events which led to the exodus from an ancient land of slavery. The Bible, centuries ago, instructed us to meet, as we do tonight, when it declared: 'And thou shalt tell thy son in that day, say: It is because of that which the Lord did for me when I came forth out of Egypt.' By this, the Bible means that young and old should gather on the eve of Passover, in order that we might relate to the children, and to all, this thrilling chapter in the history of our people."

It was indeed awesome to realize that at that very moment, all around the world, Jews were commemorating their flight from Egypt. They remembered that the angel of death "passed over" the Jewish households in Egypt which had the blood of the paschal lamb on their doorposts.

Then Eliezer called attention to the symbols on the table. "The Matzos commemorate the bread which our forefathers were compelled to eat during their hasty departure from Egypt. We use three matzos to represent the three religious groupings of the Jewish people—Kohen, Levi and Yisroayl. They are placed together to indicate the unity of the Jewish people. In unity we find our strength and power to survive.

"The second symbol is the roasted shankbone, which reminds us of the paschal lamb, a special animal sacrifice which our ancestors offered on the altar of the temple in Jerusalem on the Passover holiday.

"The third symbol is a roasted egg, which reminds us of a

second offering brought to the Temple on Passover. It was known as the 'Festival Offering,' for it was brought on each of the three festivals—Pesach, Shavuous and Succos.

"The fourth symbol is the Moror, the bitter herbs, which reminds us of the bitterness of slavery which our ancestors were compelled to endure.

"The fifth symbol is the charoses, made to resemble mortar; it is used at this time to remind us of the mortar with which our forefathers made bricks for the building of the Egyptian cities.

"The final symbol is the karpas, a green vegetable, used to remind us that Pesach coincides with the arrival of spring and the gathering of the spring harvest. Passover, in ancient times, was also an agricultural festival and an occasion on which our ancestors gave thanks for the earth's rich bounties.

"Four times in the course of this service we shall partake of wine, symbol of joy and thanksgiving. The four cups represent the fourfold promise which the Lord made to the Israelites in Egypt. In the following words, He assured them that they would be freed from servitude: 'I will bring you forth'; 'I will deliver you'; 'I will redeem you'; 'I will take you.'

"These are the symbols of Passover—echoes of the past and reminders for the present. As we partake of them, may we remember the events which they recall, and may we embody their spirit in our present-day endeavors. We shall now sanctify the holiday with the recitation of the Kiddush. Let us rise."

As the family stood together they recited from memory. "Blessed art Thou, O Lord our God, King of the universe, who createst the fruit of the vine. Blessed art Thou, O Lord, our God, who has chosen us for Thy service from among the nations, exalting us by making us holy through Thy commandments. In love hast Thou given us, O Lord our God, holidays for joy and festivals for gladness. Thou didst give us this Feast of Unleavened Bread, the season of our freedom, in commemoration of our liberation from Egypt. Thou hast chosen us for thy service from among the nations and hast sanctified us by giving us, with love and gladness, Thy holy festivals as a heritage. Blessed art Thou, O Lord, who hallowest Israel and the Festivals. Blessed art Thou, O Lord our God, King of the universe, who hast kept us in life, who has preserved us, and hast enabled us to reach this season."

The symbolic acts continued with the washing of the hands as a symbol of purification. The green vegetable was dipped into salt water and eaten to remember the tears the ancestors shed while in slavery.

Eliezer then took the three wrapped matzos from the Seder plate. He broke the middle matzoh in two, removing one half and setting it aside. This would become the "afikomen," to be eaten at the conclusion of the meal. The other half was wrapped in a napkin and "hidden." The children would later hunt for it and receive a reward.

"Lo! This is the bread of affliction," Pa continued, "the humble and simple bread which our ancestors ate in the land of Egypt. Let anyone who is hungry join us at this Seder, and let him partake of what we have to share."

"With gratitude for the blessings which we have been given," everyone said in unison, "we invite the less fortunate to share with us at this meal, and also at other times."

The one voice continued, "May the Jewish people, wherever they are, those of them still deprived of total freedom, enjoy that liberty at this time, next year." Once again everyone responded to Eliezer, "May our brethren speedily attain freedom from fear and want, and be privileged to build a symbol of peace for all the nations."

Delicious aromas from the kitchen circulated the flat as they recited the Seder together. Still to go was the asking of the four questions, the answer to the four questions, the story of Israel in the land of Egypt, the reciting of the ten plagues in Egypt, the singing of the song of gratefulness, the reciting of their personal deliverance. The bitter herb is then combined with the charoses—a sweet mixture of raisins, apples and honey. It is a reminder of how bitter slavery is, and how it can be sweetened by God's redemption.

But this Passover Joseph was waiting in anticipation for Elijah! Uncle Moishe had said that Elijah would announce the coming of the Messiah! Something had been written on Joseph's heart that day—a yearning to know the Messiah. Maybe this would be the year he would arrive. Joseph could hardly even think about the meal that was about to be served: gefilte fish, chicken soup with matzah balls, roasted chicken, potatoes, chopped liver—everything done to perfection and without a single recipe. It seemed to take more time than usual to arrive at the point when Joseph would be asked to throw open the front door and welcome in Elijah! A place had even been set for him as it was each year. Jewish legends recalled the mystical appearance of Elijah in times of trouble, to promise relief and redemption, to lift downcast spirits and to plant hope in the hearts of the downtrodden.

At last, at long last, Eliezer looked at his first-born son. "Jewish tradition states that Elijah's greatest mission shall come when the Messiah will appear on earth, to usher in the long-promised era of permanent peace and tranquillity. For it will be Elijah, the prophet, who will precede the Messiah and will announce His arrival, and with it, the arrival of freedom and peace for all men.

"On this Seder night, when we pray for freedom, we invoke the memory of the beloved Elijah. May his spirit enter our home at this hour, and every home, bringing a message of hope for the future, faith in the goodness of man, and the assurance that freedom will come to all. We now welcome Elijah, beloved guest at our Seder, as we rise."

Pa nodded and Joseph ran to throw open the front door! Would this be the year? The year when that cup of wine set for Elijah would finally be used? An eerie hush fell over the room. But no one was there.

Joseph went out into the hallway. Maybe Elijah was in another tenement flat. Maybe He was just late. He waited for several moments until Pa called him back to the table. The door was closed as it had been for years—closed on disappointed hearts who had hoped that this would be the year.

Joseph returned to the table, but he couldn't get interested in finding the afikomen, the hidden matzah. Interest failed even in the quarter he would receive, 25¢ that he could keep

and spend on anything he wanted. All he knew was that another year would have to go by until the Messiah might come.

The magical night came to an end after more prayers. The
special dishes had to be packed away again. Jewish men,
"dethroned" again until the next Passover, took up again the
burden of their lives. Meals were a letdown for weeks as the
Passover aromas lingered. Ghetto life went back to normal.

Chapter Seven

When Messiah Comes, No More Peddling!

"Ven Moshiach kumt" (When Messiah comes), Uncle Moishe always said in Yiddish. Then would come a time of peace and prosperity for all. For Joseph, it meant no more peddling!

At thirteen a Jewish boy automatically enters the state of responsibility and is Bar Mitzvad. The first thing he must then do is give allegiance to the Torah, or the Five Books of Moses. This is the central source of Jewish law and ethics; a light for thought and conduct, guiding the relationships between man and God, man and man. After he is Bar Mitzvad, a Jewish boy may be counted as one of the "minyan," the quorum of ten needed in the synagogue.

But Joseph's Bar Mitzvah left him even more spiritually desolate. Because he had to work with Pa on Saturday, the ceremony was done hurriedly one morning before school. The spiritual vacuum within him only intensified.

Life seemed to be a hopeless treadmill. Pa discouraged him from even thinking about high school. Eliezer wanted to purchase a fruit store in the Bronx and have Joseph run it. But in the meantime, he caught a crosstown bus after school each day and finished Pa's peddling route with him.

"Ven Moshiach kumt." The words had a strange ring to Joseph as he pondered them on the bus. Then there would be no more war, sickness or death.

Death—he still feared it more than anything. He could not push out the vivid scenes he had observed within his own family. Sister Leah had died that year of mastoiditis and pneumonia. The haunting smell of death still permeated their flat.

Leah had died a horrible death. She was aware in the final hours that she couldn't fight off the inevitable and still she fought for life. Those pitiful cries from Leah in the next room would forever be impressed upon him.

Golda was further weakened physically over the loss and Pa withdrew even more. And the worst part about it was that no one was sure what happened to Leah after she died: There was more uncertain speculation, more comments that "God is a just God" but that we can't know for sure about those kinds of things!

Was death just the ultimate finality? Perhaps so. It seemed that no one, from Rabbi Shapiro to Uncle Moishe, had any concrete answers to the dilemma.

Pa's horse labored up a steep hill that afternoon. The wagon was overloaded with produce and Eliezer did not dare slow him down in spite of a red light ahead. Joseph surveyed the situation with concern.

"Pa, that's a trolley route at the light," he reminded him cautiously.

Eliezer didn't answer him. It seemed that Pa withdrew more every day. He seldom shared anything with anybody; he admittedly smoked cigars to dull his mind. If he had doubts or insecurities, he kept them carefully hidden lest he be considered a weakling.

"Pa, the light," he said again. "The light ahead is red, Pa. We'd better slow down."

"Can't do it. We'll take our chances. The hill is too steep for us to stop now."

Apprehension overwhelmed Joseph as they neared the intersection. In the six years he had been peddling with his father, he had never seen him do such a foolhardy thing. But maybe the light would switch to green by the time the wagon reached the top of the hill.

"Pa, that's the clang of a trolley bell!" Joseph's voice was sharp with fear.

Eliezer sat there like he was in a trance, moving his horse on ahead. Was this the method that the angel of death had chosen for Jospeh? Was this the day and the hour that had been set aside to finish him off—that dreaded day he had feared since he saw the man jump from the tenement roof? His time had finally come! And it would be just as gruesome a fate as the one he had witnessed some years earlier!

The light seemed to be stuck on red! Another clang of the bell indicated that wagon and trolley would surely merge at the crossing!

"Please, Pa, you will kill us both!" he pleaded in terror once again.

Eliezer snapped the whip near the ear of his horse and they surged ahead. Now the trolley came into view as the wagon reached the top of the hill. The timing couldn't have been better if it had been planned. A broad side collision was inevitable and Pa didn't even look to the right or the left.

Joseph caught the expression on the face of the trolley car motorman, registering horror and unbelief that those on the wagon were so calmly going to a bloody fate.

In his stubbornness, it was clear that Eliezer was going to allow fate, chance, luck or the grace of God to determine the results. The whip snapped again in a final attempt to beat the trolley. Onlookers stopped everything and held their breath. The motorman frantically made one final attempt to at least slow down and ease the impact.

It was no use. At the moment of impact the trolley smashed into the front wheel of the wagon. Everything went flying—vegetables, fruit, wagon, horse, Pa and Joseph! The horse was sent on its stomach a full block down the street. Joseph sailed after the horse with equal speed, followed by the wagon. Pa flew in another direction.

Joseph lay pressed against the stunned horse as he watched the wagon speed his way. It would easily crush them both and every eye-witness knew it. Spectators turned away to avoid watching the gory moment of impact. That long-dreaded moment Joseph had visualized over the years was about to happen. The fear sent him into a state of semi-consciousness.

Moments later he revived to find two dozen eye-witnesses gazing down at him. By the tone of their voices, he gathered that they had just witnessed a miracle. The wheel of the wagon pressed against Joseph's hip but some mysterious force had suddenly stopped it at that very point. One witness described it as though some hand reached out of nowhere and stopped the wagon from reaching its deadly destination.

The wagon was the only casualty.

Was it the providence of God or just good fortune that spared the lives of Joseph and Eliezer and the horse? Was it, perhaps, a warning of some kind? Maybe the actual moment of death for him would be far worse than this could have been. Maybe this was merely a foretaste.

One thing was certain: no matter what, Joseph would someday get out of the peddling business! It might take years to accomplish that, along with a great deal of persistence at other endeavors such as an education.

Experiences along the way reminded him of that commitment. Peddling without a license earned him at least one night in jail with the town drunks, pimps, derelicts, gamblers and prostitutes. From that vantage point, Joseph learned that the world was a worse cesspool than he had thought.

Besides, no refined woman would want to socialize with a peddler! And as he carefully examined the various options that might bring him fulfillment, romance was now high on his list.

Chapter Eight

A Circle of Despair

For some unexplained reason, Pa's retail fruit store survived the Depression. But it was no easier to accept the death of their second daughter, Ruth. She died from mastoiditis just like Leah had. The effects of Ruth's death were predictable: Pa withdrew further, Mama was weakened even more physically, and Joseph's fear of death worsened.

The Jewish ghetto sprawled out over miles of New York City. The Leshenotskys were now able to move to the Bronx. Many immigrants had saved enough from their jobs to open their own small businesses. It was always a family affair; all members participated in the family clothing store, butcher shop, restaurant, grocery store, tailoring shop or fruit store. The days of severe poverty were over for most of them, yet financial freedom was still a decade or two away.

Golda explained their survival through the Depression as the hand of God. Pa, more skeptical, was angry that God would allow the death of his two daughters.

But Joseph could not dismiss anything in life that could possibly be providential. The latent God-awareness that had taken root in childhood blossomed more each year. Other options for giving meaning to his life were considered for a time: education, career, success, romance. But they always went full circle and came back to the beginning: peace, purpose, and life after death must rest in the hands of God alone. Every other endeavor provided only temporary answers. And eventually the hollow sound of his own emptiness would remind him that such activities provided no permanent solutions to his dilemma.

Having persuaded Eliezer to let him finish high school, he enrolled at Columbia College night school and earned the

highest grade anyone ever received in copywriting and adver-
tising. He spent his days at the fruit store and evenings in
school; somehow he sandwiched a few hours of romantic pursuit in between.

A dozen parents-turned-matchmakers hounded him. Besides being considered good husband material, Jewish tradition still encouraged parents to bring a couple together.

"Our daughter would make a good wife for you, Joseph,"
Mr. Rubin murmured, leaning over the tomatoes and speaking almost in a whisper. A mental image of his daughter Ceil
flashed through Joseph's mind. He knew she was overweight
and still had her parents' Eastern European backwardness.

"We'll set you up in business, Joseph," Mr. Segal confidently told him one afternoon. "Our Rachel is just what you
need. She has never even dated another man!" Joseph knew
why; no one wanted to take her out.

"You haven't tasted good food until you eat our Rose's
cooking," urged Mr. Kaminsky. "Her mother has taught her
to cook like we did back in the old country."

That was part of the problem; many of the girls still looked
and acted like peasant kids from Europe. Jewish girls had less
opportunity than the boys to become assimilated into the life
and culture of America. He fashioned himself as a part of the
new world intelligentsia and party society. He was a part of
the enlightened and educated generation that could not shed
old-world traditions and styles quickly enough! There was
nothing about the past, the old country, that made him cling
to it. There was nothing mystical or nostalgic about stories
from the old country that made him want to hold back from
his pursuit of happiness and fulfillment in the new world.

But one by one they filed into the fruit store, recommend-
ing their daughters to him. They each could list a dozen attri-
butes that made *their* daughter special.

But Joseph was an idealist and he would settle for nothing
less than perfection in outward beauty and in character. His
wife would have to be cultured and sophisticated, just as he
saw himself to be. She had to have new-world ways of looking
at life. He wanted an equal, not some oppressed woman whose

borders had never stretched beyond the kitchen.

Rebekah Jacobson was high on his list until he realized that she didn't look good in a bathing suit. Sadie Rosen was bow-legged. Goldie Silverman was too thin. Ruby Moskowitz was too heavy. Friede Cohen used bad grammar. Ruth Levy talked too much and Martha Lipkowitz talked too little. Rosy Greenberg was a poor dancer. But, in each case, they had fallen in love with *him*.

On and on it went until he met Milly, his ideal! She inflated his ego, and his peers would envy him if he married her. On their first date they visited a fortune-teller who said that he would marry a woman whose first name started with "M"! He knew that was confirmation that he should pursue Milly Stein. He was confident that he could get any woman he wanted with very little effort.

This time, however, *she* rejected him. In one indifferent and arrogant moment, Milly made it clear to him that Joseph Leshenotsky didn't have what it would take to get Milly Stein as a wife.

Humiliated and embarrassed, he nursed those wounds of rejection for weeks, failing to understand that he himself had inflicted those same kinds of hurts on a dozen girls.

A certain insecurity grew out of that experience, an insecurity reminding him that ego experiences couldn't satisfy that longing of the heart. Ego couldn't fill the vacuum inside of him. It had to be filled by something or someone that was a whole lot bigger than he was!

What were the signals he was missing, anyway? Was he just not hearing them, or were they deliberately kept from him as a part of some diabolical game? He never doubted there was a God; it was just that there was so little communication between them. His whole concept of God was vague. God certainly did incredible things in biblical times as Joseph had heard in Rabbi Shapiro's Bible stories—really his only exposure to the Bible. But perhaps in this twentieth century, God was resting up on some magic mushroom cloud, holding a club and taking delight in beating earthlings who were attempting to have a good time in life.

Maybe God was angered like Uncle Moishe had said years earlier! Angered because American Jews had watered down Judaism to suit their convenience, tearing apart its rituals and traditions that had gone basically unquestioned for centuries. Perhaps God was taking that anger out of Joseph's generation, since they were all a part of a massive turning away from Orthodox Judaism. Besides, it seemed that all of his peers were suffering from a similar malady centering around two questions: why am I here and where am I going?

The orthodox men would say that we were here to study the Torah, to worship God, to serve our fellowman and to pray for the return of the Messiah. Then, if our lives were primarily characterized by good works, we stood a good chance of entering heaven.

But twentieth-century living was hardly conducive to the orthodox philosophy of good and honest words and deeds. After all, this was a dog-eat-dog society. One got ahead by trampling on those in his way. You cheated and lied in business or you would never make it in the new world. You padded your pocketbook and advanced yourself in ways that were immoral, to say the least, and often illegal.

If God was keeping a score sheet, Joseph and his peers wouldn't even make it up the first rung of that ladder to heaven! And if that destination wasn't possible, then what awaited a person who had lost his inheritance in heaven? That nagging question hadn't left his mind now for more than a decade!

When Yom Kippur time rolled around he was determined to gain some spiritual insights and understanding or else not waste his time fasting and praying.

Yom Kippur, the Jewish Day of Atonement, is the holiest day of the year. It is a day of fasting, praying and beating the chest to atone for the sins of that year. No food or drink may touch the lips, and no earthly concerns are to enter the mind as one stands before God.

Prayers are repeated in the synagogue all day long. All prayers include the confession of sin. They are recited privately for God to hear and also repeated in unison, acknowledging mutual responsibility for one another. Prayers were led by the

Rabbi, who often sounded like he was imploring a seemingly reluctant God to forgive the sins of the people.

But even before the Day of Atonement the people are urged to make up the wrongs committed to fellowmen, for without reconciliation among men there can be no forgiveness from God. The Rabbis urge everyone to seek out his enemy, showing generosity and forgiveness. Only then is one really prepared for Yom Kippur.

But, admittedly, many involved themselves only out of duty, obedience and respect to elders. Joseph was aware that there could be little, if any, atoning merit when handled with such weak motives. Besides, no matter *how* much he followed the traditions of Yom Kippur, he never felt that one ounce of guilt or sin had been removed from him. Nor was the hope of heaven any closer to him.

And it was questionable whether anyone who wasn't from the old country understood much that was said during Yom Kippur services. Prayers were repeated all day in Hebrew; even after eight years of Hebrew School, Joseph still didn't know what he was saying when he repeated those mechanical prayers. Nor did very many others of his generation.

In one last attempt to find his answers within Judaism, he purchased a Hebrew prayer book that had the English translation next to the Hebrew. Maybe this would help him put together some of the missing pieces of the puzzle.

As had been the custom, Pa purchased synagogue seats for himself and his son. Joseph was intrigued by the fact that each year Eliezer placed himself next to the wall. But this time realization dawned on Joseph: Pa wanted to turn his face to the wall as he broke down and cried during each Yom Kippur service. This was the way he poured out his heart to God over the many disappointments he had known in life. Joseph was reminded of the Jews in Palestine at the Wailing Wall.

No one spoke as hundreds of people entered the synagogue, a holy hush permeating the place. The women were confined to the balcony while the men sat as families below.

Joseph felt it best not to mention the Hebrew-English prayer book he had in his pocket. There had been no time to study it and he didn't want to call special attention to it by bringing it out early. For once, however, he waited with expectancy for the service to begin, for this year he might gain some answers.

The cantor sang eloquently as usual. Everyone swayed to the rhythm of the prayers when they stood—prayers for forgiveness, holiness, and mercy. There seemed to be a new aura about this Yom Kippur. Maybe it was the messianic hope, or maybe just an inner pride that they had all survived the Depression and better times were ahead.

Joseph would have liked to have looked deep within the heart of these outwardly pious men. What really was Judaism to them? Was it messianic expectations or was it ethnic pride, tradition, and a kind of Zionism that was being expounded by a woman named Golda Meir? No one was quite sure who she was, but anyone who heard her knew that the world would hear more and more about her and her cause, Palestine. And no one was fully sure what Zionism was, but it sounded so Jewish that it must be good—at least good for the poor Jews of Europe; not so good perhaps, for those who had made it in America. There were just too many comforts to give up should one consider settling in the wasteland of Palestine.

But Golda Meir sold Palestine so well that thousands of Jews from *all* economic classes began to set aside money to assist her cause of a Jewish homeland. A man by the name of Theodore Herzl had promoted it before she did. Few Jews had responded to his call, however. In another decade, world Jewry would lament their sluggishness in responding to the call of the Zionists.

The service progressed that afternoon with Joseph following along in the new prayer book. Pa seemed too lost in his own anguish to notice it.

"And for the sins for which we owe a burnt offering," the Rabbi read in Hebrew, "and for the sins for which we owe a sin-offering; for the sins for which we owe an offering according to our ability; and for the sins for which we owe a trespass offering for certain guilt and a trespass offering for doubtful guilt; and for the sins for which we deserve the punishment of forty stripes; and for the sins for which we deserve death by the hand of God; and for the sins for which we deserve the punishment of excision, and of being childless; and for all these, O God of forgiveness, forgive us, pardon us, grant us atonement. And for the sins for which we deserve the four kinds of death inflicted by the Court of Law: stoning, burning, beheading, and strangling. . . . "

The Rabbi went on in Hebrew but Joseph no longer heard, stunned by that which he just read in English. He looked at it again silently: "And for the sins for which we deserve the four kinds of death . . . stoning, burning, beheading and strangling. . . . "

It was true! The dreadful sin of which mankind was capable warranted one of those kinds of punishment! *Unless* there was some kind of atonement, some sin-bearer. But *who* or *what* could it be that would *adequately* atone for the wretchedness of mankind? Certainly not good works! One could *never* do enough good works to pacify an angry God. And how could a one-day fast on Yom Kippur atone for sins so dreadful that God would pronounce such a just and severe punishment for them?

Why hadn't he been told all of this earlier in life? Now at his age he could total up a thousand known sins; but what about all the *unknown* sins and all those he had probably forgotten?

One thing was certain: there was clearly no hope or assurance of eternity in heaven! There could be no certainty of life after death because there was no adequate sin-bearer for a lifetime of sins.

A heavy cloud of depression settled over Joseph. As if in a hypnotic trance, he slowly made his way out of the synagogue as a hundred annoyed faces followed him. One simply didn't leave a front row seat during a Yom Kippur service and cause disruption. But at that point, he didn't care if he or even Pa incurred the wrath of the men of the synagogue.

He spoke to himself as he walked out into the brisk October air, "Man has no hope. No hope. *Nothing* can atone for the dreadful sins we've committed. We're all doomed because there is no sin-bearer."

He headed for a park across from the synagogue. Maybe it

would be better if he had never known this. No wonder the world was on a treadmill that encouraged everyone to grab what they could now. It was clear one couldn't take anything along when death came, since no one knew where he was going.

The only certainty was that four options lay ahead: stoning, burning, beheading or strangling. It was all there in the Hebrew prayer book! All the members of the synagogue had just read it without question in Hebrew as they had for years.

Why had he rocked the boat by buying the English translation? Ignorance could have meant a certain degree of bliss. Besides, maybe God would have more mercy on those who did not know this.

Sitting on a park bench, he buried his head in his hands. What kind of a God would do such an evil trick on humanity? Certainly not the Jewish God. Even the pagan tribes buried away in some remote jungle had some place of eternal reward. How could civilized man—Jews no less, with whom God had made a covenant—have no hope of eternity and no proper method of atonement? Sacrifices had not been offered since Bible times.

Man could endure anything if he had hope. The Jews had endured thousands of years of slavery, oppression and pogrom; and they had survived, Joseph concluded, because they had hope.

But upon what was that hope based? Speculation? The good outweighing the bad, so that the scales of eternity would be tipped in the end?

Nothing made much sense. It was an exercise in futility to play mental gymnastics with God and good works, ritual and tradition, and never know *for sure* that anything was accomplished by it! Perhaps it was even futile to pin one's hopes and dreams on some messianic deliverance from it all. The world was in too big a mess to be salvaged by any such Messiah.

Or was it? Maybe such a one as the Messiah was the *only* hope of the world. Everything and everyone else was a collosal disappointment! No one lived up to expectations. Everyone was out for himself. Big people stepped on little people who, in turn, stepped on wives or children. It was a game of survival of the fittest, or the strongest, or the most cunning or clever, or the one who had the most connections.

And Joseph knew that he was no exception to all of that. It was that kind of honesty that forced him to look at his own wretchedness and emptiness. He was willing to admit, inwardly at least, that he was playing the same kind of con game with humanity to advance his own cause, pursuits and ego. People were stepping-stones on his path to success, and it mattered very little if some were crushed along the way. It was their own fault for not playing the same kind of a game.

Peers reinforced such thinking. Sufficiently trouncing someone on your own mad pursuit to the top in the American way of life earned you a pat on the back at the very least. And maybe "Salesman of the Year" or a blurb in *Who's Who in America?*

Society was geared that way, wasn't it? Didn't that make it right? Maybe not.

If it was right, why did his whole inner being want to be turned inside out for a massive cleansing? A cleansing from every evil thought and sin that warranted that stoning, burning, beheading and strangling!

Such thoughts were never far from his mind. Even sleep proved to be a dreaded experience. Nightmares of death flashed back and forth across his subconscious like frantic bolts of lightning. There was no escape from those dreams depicting bizarre death scenes.

Awake or asleep, he was certain that he was on a one-way collision course to some destination where he would be sentenced to a painful death. And there was no escape unless something, or someone, could cover the multitude of selfish sins that surrounded him.

No escape. Life—a circle with despair at the beginning and the end. An endless round of guilt that left him tied in chains, perhaps never to be unlocked, even in eternity.

Chapter Nine
No Real Answers

Sarah was an attractive, innocent girl from the country, totally uncorrupted by the big city. She was Joe's ideal; she fit all the requirements he had mentally outlined for a wife. However, she didn't share his intense spiritual search and hunger for God.

But she was able to deaden some inner anxieties Joe had been experiencing: his mother's failing health, his own quest for spiritual reality, and the frustration and fear over his floundering business which shifted precariously with the economy.

He'd grown frustrated as a salesman for a paper and twine company and decided to launch a small paper, twine and office supply business of his own.

So Joe's inner turmoil was eased slightly when he married Sarah in 1936. At the same time he changed his family name to Lessin.

But a year later when son Donald arrived, many of those fears and insecurities returned full force. At the time, his business was tottering on the brink of collapse. Hitler had been making rumblings in Europe and war clouds on the horizon created an uncertain economic future for the small businessman.

Joe was forced to take a second job as an all-night cashier at Tofenetti's Restaurant in Manhatten. Even these long hours didn't allow him to work himself to the point where he was too numb to think. And his deep love for Sarah and Don wasn't the cure-all that he hoped it would be, either.

He began to consider the fact that a remedy for his dilemma probably didn't exist. Perhaps it was God's will that earthlings wallow in uncertainty, doubt and even misery, with no assurance about anything, including life after death.

American Jewry was now getting letters from Europe with news of increased persecution. For America's Jews who had fled that kind of a scene a generation or so earlier, they found that they experienced terrible flashbacks of their own horror. Joe's elders were all too familiar with pogroms; but news of **genocide (race annihilation), concentration camps and ovens** that cremated countless numbers of people was almost beyond comprehension. Many American Jews simply refused to believe it. They were sure that America would *never* allow, even on foreign shores, such a thing to happen! It must be exaggerated rumor. (It was some years before the curtain of history was removed and the devastation of the Holocaust unveiled.)

Perhaps the Zionists were right after all. Maybe Palestine was the only workable solution to the problem of the wandering, unwanted Jew. A homeland was needed to receive those who had been in exile for so long. So far they had been driven out of every country but America. And the homeland wasn't needed merely for protection; it was needed to restore a feeling of community and spiritual and ethnic oneness—in the place where it all began centuries ago.

One thing was clear: America could not take care of the world's Jewish population. Already she was faced with a dilemma: should she admit thousands more Jewish refugees, or should she reject them and subject them to a lifetime of oppression in other lands?

In an unusual way, Europe's incarcerated Jews finally brought together America's bickering Jewish population. Able to set aside tremendous political and religious differences, they mobilized enormous financial resources for those in Europe. Some had connections that might be able to put political pressure on European governments. The futile hope was that this would improve the living conditions for those Jewish people and make it unnecessary for them to emigrate to America, further complicating the economy.

The Holocaust made more obscure the Jewish spiritual dilemma, of which Joe Lessin's questioning mentality was representative. He kicked around a half-dozen related questions every day as the startling facts trickled into America. What kind of a God would allow this to happen? Where was God when the Cyclone B gas was turned on in two dozen death camps? Where was the outcry from the world's Gentile population, that vast nameless and faceless segment of humanity that called themselves the "silent majority"? How could Germany's "Christian" population condone such policies, attending church on Sunday with an unburdened conscience? It appeared that the Gentiles were up to their usual behavior again, at least in the eyes of most Jews: they worshipped the Jewish Jesus, but through their silence and apathy condoned the slaughter of Europe's Jewish population.

And the biggest question of all still remained hopelessly unanswered: where was that Messianic Deliverer whom they had waited for so long? Why was He silent at a time when His people needed Him so desperately? For centuries they had waited for Him to come, and never was the need so urgent as it was now, with Hitler marching through city after city, proudly posting banners that proclaimed "Judenrein" (free of Jews).

Joe prepared to leave for Tofenetti's for his all-night shift. He felt unusually tired, but then he'd worked countless number of hours that week between his two jobs. When he had finished at the restaurant each morning at 8:00 a.m. he caught a bus to his small office where he ran the office supply business. He snatched a few hours of sleep wherever he could.

Sarah noticed that he was unusually pensive as he prepared to leave that evening.

"Something's wrong, isn't it?" she inquired intuitively.

He hesitated. "The fear is back," he finally admitted.

"What fear?"

"You know, about death and all." His voice trailed off.

"I think you're too negative and too gloomy," Sarah said. "You take everything so seriously."

"So death is serious business, Sarah."

Several seconds of silence followed as Joe collected his thoughts. Finally he spoke up again. "Sarah, if God is a reality like I'm sure that He is, then sin is also a reality. And if that is the case, then heaven and hell are, too. So am I too serious just because I want to know to which place I'm going?"

"So you die, you die," Sarah said casually, shrugging her shoulders. "All of humanity shares that fate. So you think *you* should be an exception or something? I'm not afraid to die, Joe. Look, you take what you can get out of life while you have it."

"That philosophy has never lessened the fear in me. It's simplistic and it's a pat answer that just doesn't work for me. It ultimately drives men to all the wrong answers in life. They lead miserable lives and die miserable deaths and nobody seems to know for sure what happens to them after that."

There was this built-in communication gap with Sarah because of their differing awareness of spiritual truth.

"Sarah," Joe said as he put his coat on, "there are days when I want to die just so I can stop thinking about death. That sounds crazy, doesn't it?"

Sarah nodded her head wryly in obvious agreement.

"Talk to God about it all," she suggested, not sarcastically.

"I've tried, Sarah. I can't get through to Him. Maybe it's my fault. The orthodox men look and think in an outdated manner. Very little is questioned, and the way our ancestors operated is still okay with them. Sometimes I think that they park their brain somewhere and just rehash what their fathers and grandfathers taught them. But they have few doubts about God, death and eternity. They have some kind of blind faith that God is just and that He will make the balances come out even, as long as we study Torah, do good works and love God and our fellowman. But they can't be *absolutely sure* about life after death. Maybe—just maybe, their good deeds weren't really good enough; maybe they brushed their teeth on Yom Kippur and swallowed some water, breaking their fast and angering God. They have to work so hard to make sure that God doesn't slam the gate shut on that judgment day.

"Besides," Joe continued, opening the door to leave, "they kept me from reading the Yom Kippur service in English for twenty years. I've often wondered how much else they have kept from me."

He left earlier than usual that night. He wanted to be alone and try to sort through some issues. He recognized that he had begun to escape into a make-believe world. He tried to lose himself at the movies or in music; he never allowed himself to be alone anymore, but surrounded himself with people and conversation, no matter how meaningless that conversation might be. These activities kept him from thinking, for his thoughts ultimately brought fear and insecurity upon him.

Besides, Joe Lessin hadn't wanted to remind himself of the paradox that he was: a totally free man hopelessly locked in chains and behind bars of his own making. What made that worse was the underlying realization that his liberation was available; a key was hidden somewhere, but he couldn't seem to find it. His attempt at once more making sense of it all during his walk were no more fruitful than before.

It was unusually cold as he left Tofenetti's that next morning. Joe nearly lost his breath each time a cold rush of wind hit him. The fatigue wrapped around him like a cloud this morning and each step felt like forced labor.

New York City in the month of March seldom lifts one's depression. Soot-stained snow in patches alongside neglected garbage fit right in with Joe's view of life. New York at the end of the Depression was still an interesting contrast of old and new. Gone were the peddlers' carts, replaced by the frantic whine of subways, trolleys, buses and automobiles. But the constant influx of immigrants, many of whom still looked like they stepped out of another century, gave an old-world color to the city. On any given block in New York, one could hear a jumble of a half-dozen languages.

Joe caught a bus to his office that morning to escape the cold. A wave of nausea had almost overcome him, but he felt it was fatigue complicated by the exhaust from the street traffic. But the sickness definitely worsened as the bus wound its way toward the other end of Manhatten to his one-room office. Fortunately he had been able to get the last remaining seat on the bus as rush-hour commuters filled it up quickly—just as well since his symptoms worsened almost immediately. Suddenly a sharp pain tore through his chest and knocked the breath out of him. He tried to muffle his gasps for air. To distract onlookers, he turned his head toward the window lest anyone see his distorted face. Grabbing hold of the seat in front of him, he squeezed it until his hand was nearly white. He was either too proud or embarrassed to ask for help and no one offered it, all a part of that New York apathy.

How could a man barely thirty years old be suffering a heart attack? Joe wondered. He rubbed his chest, hoping to ease the pain.

Maybe he should pray, but how? How does one address a God he's never met and doesn't understand? Besides, what had Joe ever done for God that should make God want to return a favor? God probably operated with the same set of principles that man does: you do for me and I'll do for you.

Then again, perhaps this was God's way of punishing Joe Lessin for a lifetime of sin and selfishness. He wouldn't go by burning, stoning, beheading or strangling, but by a heart attack at a ridiculously young age!

Trying to pray anyway, believing what his elders had said about God being just, Joe hoped that maybe God would look with more favor upon him simply because he had *earnestly* sought Him for so many years.

"If you're there," he whispered, "help me, somehow."

That was it. The Almighty would have to understand that at the moment Joe wasn't a man of eloquence; he was desperate.

The pain worsened, however, and his breathing became more difficult. This was what it was like to die! The fear of that dreadful moment which had occupied both his waking and sleeping hours was about to become reality!

He wrapped his coat around himself more tightly and angled his whole body towards the window so no one would see his struggle. Somehow he had to get off the bus and catch a subway to his apartment.

The world rushed by him outside of the bus window, but his eyes couldn't focus on anything. He continued to rub his chest and mutter a weak, "O God. O God." Someone once told him that God had a lot of mercy. Just maybe it would be shown to him now at his moment of need.

The pain suddenly eased and he decided to exit. After a few awkward steps toward the door, however, he had to stop and balance himself between several people. The bus was so crowded that no one thought anything about it. It took him nearly ten minutes to work himself to the back door of the bus. Too weak to push the buzzer, he simply waited until someone else exited and followed.

Another blast of late-winter air hit him as he got off. The nearest subway station was two blocks away. Every few steps he had to pause and catch his breath, leaning on a building or sitting on a bus bench. But even during his pain and confusion Joe was aware that some supernatural hand seemed to be keeping him from total collapse. Maybe God wasn't keeping score so carefully after all. Or was it merely his own stiff-necked stubbornness which allowed him to move on.

He reached the subway entry; ahead of him was a long flight down the stairs. After each step there was a momentary pause for air in an effort to ease his pain.

Just one place was left on a bench on the subway platform. Great gaps of time he couldn't account for as he drifted in and out of reality. He finally eased his way into a car. Was it God or was it his own inner drive that brought him back to consciousness twenty minutes later at the right subway stop? Was it God or was it some invisible time or space machine that got him up three flights of stairs to his apartment?

He collapsed in a heap on the threshold.

For six weeks Joe Lessin was confined to total bed rest. Another six months of convalescence was spent on a farm in Connecticut. His body was worn out by long hours with little sleep, and his nervous system had been shattered by fear, uncertainty and the dread of the unknown. Added to that was the frustration of thirty years with no real answers to his searching questions.

Chapter Ten

Where Was God . . . ?

The warm California breezes were a vast improvement over New York's cold, damp air. The warmer climate would be better for Joe and had been prescribed along with the barbiturates. But the teaspoon of liquid barbiturates three times a day quickly became a tablespoon three times a day. Finally Joe was drinking it straight out of the bottle; then heavy sleeping pills were added to the routine.

His entire family had moved West, including a new son, Roy, with Eliezer and Golda. He had made a little profit selling his paper, twine and office supply business back in New York and he hoped to start a similar business in Southern California.

America's Jewish population was now sprawling across the nation, with the largest concentration in the major cities of the East, in Florida, and west to Chicago, San Francisco and Los Angeles. Other poor ethnic groups began to occupy those same tenement flats that had housed the "hordes of Jewish aliens" a generation earlier.

California was as yet not quite so corrupt as New York. Frowned on were the cut-throat business methods that were a way of life back in New York. So getting his business going was a real struggle for Joe.

And a steady work routine was still difficult for him. The abuses of the barbiturates and the sleeping pills made getting up in the morning difficult. Work days were kept short—perhaps four hours. Mounting financial problems were inevitable. And the financial and health complications quickly sent Joe and Sarah's marriage into a tailspin, resulting in deeper depression and more pills. . . .

Tranquillity and peace were as elusive as butterflies in a

spring garden. It was a great disappointment to realize that his new Southern California life-style was not the answer he had hoped it would be. There were a few good times, and the ache inside of him was dulled on occasion. But the good times were so temporary that he could only conclude that happiness, peace and fulfillment were simply *not* attainable through relationships, possessions or circumstances. If these were possible for Joe, they must be acquired *in spite* of life's circumstances. But so far no one, even the spiritual leaders within the Jewish community, had ever provided him with the missing pieces of that puzzle.

The result was that he took out his frustration and anger most frequently on Sarah and the boys. He couldn't seem to stop himself from inflicting emotional hurt on them. Somebody else in this world had to feel as miserable as Joe Lessin. If, as it appeared, no one had any answers, then misery must have company—they would all wallow in it together.

There seemed to be varying degrees of distress among his peers. Sam Sheiner and his family had also moved from the Bronx and settled not far from the Lessins in Los Angeles. Joe frequently talked over his frustrations with Sam, though both generally concluded with mutual uncertainty about life.

But Sam had little inner drive for any kind of God-consciousness. He was one of the many Jewish men and women who had finally abandoned the faith of their fathers. Even the watered-down reform branch of Judaism became a burden to them.

For some, political radicalism was all that was left of the religious spirit which motivated their ancestors. Liberal politics and atheism seemed to walk hand in hand into the spiritual void remaining in this growing segment of Judaism. The ranks of the Jewish socialists and communists grew continually. Many had simply become disillusioned with America in spite of the haven of safety it offered. To others, embracing communism was a way of clinging to the old country from which they had fled and for which some still longed. The destruction of the Czar by the communists had meant some temporary freedom for the Jews in that part of the world.

Others saw socialism and communism as the means to developing a classless society, forever doing away with the downtrodden masses—a group of which every Jew felt he had been a part.

The Holocaust now played a major role in that idea. It would forever leave its mark on all generations of Jews and color their view of racism and war. But an even stronger influence on Jewish thought was materialism. Ghetto life had been tolerable to them because as children they had known nothing else. *Their* children, however, would be pampered and cradled in affluence.

A whole generation of shrewd young businessmen emerged. Their fathers had advanced out of the ghettos and into their own small shops, "ma and pa" stores; but this generation would produce some of the nation's top doctors, lawyers and business executives. And "family money" hardly ever put them through school; hard work and that uncanny Jewish drive pushed them to the top.

And they moved to the top too quickly to suit some Americans. Feeling intimidated, their lack of understanding caused them to refuel some fires of anti-Semitism in spite of the recent atrocities in Europe. To the Gentile the Jew always has been an enigma, their clannishness offensive and their intellectual capacity making outsiders insecure.

On the other hand, Jews could not ignore the fact that most of the world had looked on indifferently as one-third of world Jewry was annihilated in Europe. It was, of course, a repeat performance of what preceding generations had experienced, though the setting and the methods may have changed. Persecution now took the shape of unfair discrimination, of verbal abuse.

Whatever the methods and motives, such practices did little to ease that inner depression so characteristic of Joe and many of his peers. So their anger turned inward, which added to their despondency and frustration.

Now Joe was actually entertaining ideas of murder and suicide. To escape the fear of death once and for all, he seriously considered taking his own life. For brief moments he could find that even amusing. Basically a coward and fond of some comforts in life, Joe's concept of such finality—no doubt accompanied by some pain—was contradictory to his nature. But he was helplessly in bondage to the total meaning of death; he even considered the murder of Sarah, Don and Roy.

Sam Sheiner had few answers to life, but he listened well. Having a genuine concern for Joe, his buddy from the Bronx, he could effectively humor him and yet be frank with him.

They talked of old times or dreamed of better days ahead. Their heritage was all they really had in common, for Sam was an atheist and Joe was still in pursuit of God, though admittedly more passively than in previous years. But that basic difference made them come at issues from opposite directions; somehow they managed to merge somewhere along the way.

From politics to morality, few topics were not dissected by Sam and Joe as they met at Barney's in East Los Angeles for coffee. They tried to polish their ghetto philosophy and sound like representatives of middle-class America. They wanted others to look at them and realize that Joe Lessin and Sam Sheiner had climbed from lower class to middle class and that they planned to rise still higher.

But Joe brought God into too many conversations, according to Sam.

"People like you are unrealistic dreamers," Sam insisted that afternoon. "You look at the filth and the rottenness of the world and you try to fit a God into it. Can't you see that if there is a God, by now He has given up on humanity?"

Joe sipped his coffee and tried to block out the chatter and laughter that were always too loud at Barney's.

"Maybe it's the other way around," Joe replied. "Maybe we've given up on God. Maybe He still wants a reconciliation with man."

"Joe, since I met you at your pa's fruit store back in the Bronx, you've been looking for ethereal answers to your life. You could never just accept that things happen without some celestial force controlling them. Tell me, would God have let our people be exterminated in Hitler's ovens? Isn't the concept of God that He is all-powerful and that He is greater than the Czars and the Hitlers of the world? So tell me, Joe Lessin, where was God when the six million died?"

"I don't know, Sam. Somehow I think He was there with them."

"And now you're gonna tell me that maybe God is at the bottom of this crazy death-wish you have? You've got some God, Lessin, who will put up with a 'shnook' like you! I mean, what kind of a God deserves a guy like you who hangs such ideas on Him?"

Joe didn't feel like arguing or even like having a healthy debate this day. He stared blankly into his coffee cup.

"Look, Joe," Sam continued more compassionately, "why don't you and I get away for a weekend? We'll take a run up to Vegas; maybe we'll get lucky and win a few bucks and we can forget our troubles for a while. You know, we'll take in a few shows and really live it up! What do you say?"

"I don't know, Sam. I don't think—"

Sam wouldn't let him finish.

"Look, if nothing else, the climate will be good for you. It's a lot warmer this time of year in Vegas."

"I just don't know, Sam."

"Come on," Sam pleaded once more. "Let loose and quit taking life so seriously. Vegas is a great place to forget things and just let go."

"Okay, Sam. Just for the weekend."

"Good! It will help you forget a lot of things and, who knows, maybe we'll get rich quick."

If it were only that easy, Joe thought to himself. Family, health and financial pressures could not be so flippantly tossed aside. They had a way of resurfacing at inconvenient times. Other parties involved were not quick to let him forget. Sarah was growing more distant and son Donald was showing early signs of the same kind of fear that Joe had felt towards his dad. Creditors hounded him, poor health continuing to play havoc with his work routine. When he was candid with himself, which was often, he realized that he was involved in an alarming abuse of barbiturates and sleeping pills.

The idea that one weekend in Las Vegas could erase those

issues was absurd; but for Sam's sake, Joe would try to enjoy the weekend. The most he could lose might be a couple hundred dollars; maybe he would get lucky, in fact, and win a few. Then he could pay off some creditors. He would try to relax and enjoy himself like Sam suggested.

Joe told himself that he was embarrassed because he hadn't yet seen Vegas. Afterall, he saw himself as an avante-garde member of society; not as radical as some but, nonetheless, open to new experiences, ideas and risks. He found it often left awkward gaps in conversations because he had not experienced Las Vegas!

Everyone talked about it, and surely it was a social disgrace not to have been there.

Joe tuned out Sam and the din that surrounded them at Barney's. Staring hypnotically at the cup he held in his hand, he felt powerless to push out the thoughts that surfaced again. He would have one final fling in Las Vegas next weekend, then return home and murder Sarah and the boys, and then kill himself.

Chapter Eleven

Can Any Good Come Out of Las Vegas?

The bright lights of the city could be seen from several miles away, lighting up the sky. They seemed to beckon Sam and Joe to speed up just in case they might miss even a few moments of their weekend hoopla.

Las Vegas pulsated with life and good times even if there were some there who had lost their financial shirts at the gambling tables.

The Desert Inn Hotel bathed its guests in a kind of luxury neither of them had known. Most of the hotel guests appeared to be like Sam and Joe—middle-class American folks on a weekend adventure that might hopefully net them some cash and good times or could send them further into debt. And yet nobody seemed too worried about the latter.

And it was an easy place to forget about one's home. Singles became couples within hours. For a day or a week, everybody lived daringly and did a lot of things they shouldn't and normally wouldn't. As long as it was just a Las Vegas lifestyle, some rationalized, and not the all-American way of life, nobody seemed to be too concerned.

The sounds of Las Vegas were unique: coins rattling together as they poured out of slot machines; dice tumbling over tables and generating enthusiasm or groans from dozens of players and spectators; cocktail glasses banging together to celebrate a good day at the gambling tables. And there were the jaded who made no sound at all, sitting in stoic silence whether winning or losing.

Joe was unusually quiet as they checked into the hotel and found their way to their room. But Sam had enough enthusiasm for both of them. More excited than a kid on Christmas

Eve, he had already thought of all the ways he would spend the money he planned on winning.

They eventually made their way to one of the smoke-filled gambling rooms in the Desert Inn. About a dozen people stood around twenty different gambling tables. Most had cold, hard faces; others showed that they'd had a bad day at the tables. A few arrogantly put all their winning money down on another gambling table, greedily hoping to double their money. Somewhere in the distance somebody let out a scream after hitting the jackpot in a slot machine.

Sam pointed to a table that seemed to have room for some more players. The players were anxiously counting their chips, eager to multiply them.

"What do you say, Joe?" Sam asked enthusiastically. "Let's start our lucky streak over there."

Joe nodded his agreement.

Neither had more gambling experience than an occasional poker game, and yet Sam marched confidently up to the table as though he were an expert. Sam poked an elbow into Joe. "I want you to really let loose tonight," Sam exhorted. "I want you to forget about Sarah and the business and everything else and just concentrate on those dice. And I want you to shoot up a prayer or two to that God of yours, if you are so sure He exists. Tell Him we want to win some money this weekend. Okay?"

After exchanging some money for colored chips, the two joined the game.

With his usual confidence, Sam elbowed his way into the group around the table and slapped $20 worth of chips down. An elegantly dressed man in dark glasses coolly reached for the chips with a long pole and placed them on an appropriate spot on the table. Then, the way he had done a hundred times that day, he mechanically explained the procedure to the new players. The success or failure of the game lay in the dice. Everyone had three throws of the dice; accordingly, one stood to double his money or lose it all.

"I feel beginner's luck coming over us!" Sam raved enthusiastically to anybody who might want to hear.

Eagerly shaking the dice, Sam tossed them. Sure enough—one toss of the dice and he doubled his money! A few at the table slapped Sam on the back and dug deeper into their own pockets for money to buy more chips. It was *too* easy; Joe was seeing how Vegas could charm most anyone.

"What did I tell you!" Sam exclaimed. "Joe, you stick with me and your money worries will be over. I can just feel it!"

Somebody handed the dice to Joe next. His hands began to sweat as the two smooth cubes lay in his palm. Maybe this whole thing was making him too nervous for his bad heart and emotional system.

"Throw the dice!" someone said impatiently.

Joe continued to stand quietly for several seconds, unsure of the reason for his hesitation.

"Yea, come on, Joe!" Sam chimed in.

Joe put his chips down on the table and shook the dice in his hand. Just as he was about to toss them, he heard someone say, "Joe, get away from the table right now."

He stopped the dice toss and looked around in confusion.

"Who said that?" he inquired, alarmed.

"Said what?" Sam asked.

"Who told me to get away from the table?"

"Lessin, come on, pal!" Sam said obviously annoyed and embarrassed by his friend. "Play the game!"

"Sam, I can't. I don't know what's wrong, but I have to get out of here." He returned the dice to the table and retrieved his chips.

"Joe! Lady luck is with us tonight!" Sam protested from the side of his mouth. "How can you do this to me? You're putting a damper on this whole weekend and we just got started!"

"You play, Sam. I'm going to our room. Like I said, I can't explain it, but I heard somebody tell me to get away from this table."

"He's been under a lot of pressure," Sam explained to the others apologetically. They shook their heads, more in disgust than in sympathy.

Joe pushed his way through the crowd and headed for the room. He was puzzled and alarmed by that voice. Had it been audible? Had it been an inner voice?

One thing was certain—he had to find a distraction. The

experience had been too unnerving to sit and ponder. There wasn't a thing to read in the hotel room, so he decided to write a letter to friends back in New York. Yes, a letter would take his mind off the situation. Every hotel room has stationery.

Drawer after drawer was empty of any paper. Opening the last drawer he realized something was pushed into the back. Reaching in, he discovered a book. Relieved at finding something to do, Joe didn't care just so he could forget the experience of a few moments earlier!

He pulled it out into the light.

"A Bible!" he exclaimed out loud. Joe had never read a Bible—only the Hebrew prayer book he'd purchased years earlier back in New York. An unexplicable quickening within him returned.

Propping some pillows up on the bed, Joe made himself comfortable, ready to look at his discovery. He saw that it had been placed in the hotel by the Gideons. Opening it randomly, he turned to Proverbs. He began to read "He that hath knowledge spareth his words: and a man of understanding is of an excellent spirit. Even a fool, when he holdeth his peace, is counted wise: and he that shutteth his lips is esteemed a man of understanding."

"He that goeth about as a talebearer revealeth secrets: therefore meddle not with him that flattereth with his lips." Joe was amazed at the wisdom found in that particular book of the Bible! He agreed with nearly every verse. He knew that the philosophy found in them was accurate. Whoever authored those words was a wise man!

He pored through the Proverbs for hours, almost amused when he found the places where the author shared Joe's philosophy of life. He still had his nose buried in the Bible when Sam returned around 2:00 a.m.

Rolling his eyes in disgust as he saw his friend glued to a book on their expensive weekend, Sam exclaimed, "What! We come all the way to Vegas and spend twenty bucks a night on a room so that you can stick your nose into a book? You're something else, pal!"

"Sam, it's a Bible! I found a Bible. Have you ever read one? I haven't."

"I won over $200 tonight. What do you have to show for your time here? Joe, I'm not interested in your Bible tonight or at any other time for that matter!"

"Sam, listen to this." Joe ignored Sam's sarcasm. " 'These seven are an abomination unto the Lord. A proud look, a lying tongue, and hands that shed innocent blood, an heart that deviseth wicked imaginations, feet that be swift in running to mischief, a false witness that speaketh lies, and he that soweth discord among brethren.' And hear this," he went on enthusiastically, " 'He that refuseth instruction despiseth his own soul: but he that heareth reproof getteth understanding. The fear of the Lord is the instruction of wisdom: and before honor is humility' " (Prov. 6:16-19; 15:31-33).

Sam walked into the bathroom and slammed the door, but Joe kept reading, through the closed door.

"Sam, it says in here," Joe said more loudly, "that there is an escape from fear. 'But whoso hearkeneth unto me shall dwell safely, and shall be quiet from fear of evil.' Who do you suppose that's referring to, Sam? God, maybe?"

There was no reply from the bathroom.

"This one is good, too," Joe continued. " 'A fool's mouth is his destruction, and his lips are the snare of his soul.' "

Sam blustered out and tried to reason with Joe again. "You're not going to sit here for three days and read, are you?" he pleaded. "How about taking in a show tomorrow night? There are some great acts in town. Look, you don't have to gamble if you don't want to, but at least take in a show with me tomorrow night."

"I'll see, Sam."

"Why me?" Sam asked the ceiling in disgust. "Why do I have to end up in Vegas with a bookworm?" Pulling some pillows over his head, he attempted to drown out Joe's chatter.

Joe continued to read on into the night. The more he read, the more intrigued he became. How had he gone through eight years of Hebrew School and more than twenty years in the synagogue and not read a Bible? Joe finally thought to check on who wrote the Proverbs and was thrilled to learn that it was King Solomon, David's son! No wonder it was so terrific!

A faint glimmer of dawn began to show before he finally

put the Bible down. He felt unusually calm inside, even rested, in spite of the fact that he'd been up most of the night. He'd even forgotten to take his barbiturates.

As he thought over what he had read, he was tempted to look at the last part of the book, the New Testament. He was more than curious about Jesus, the Gentile God, the one the Jews had always been accused of killing. Joe couldn't remember ever hearing anything positive about Jesus or His followers. Eliezer and Golda had often told him stories of forced conversions and baptism in Russia by the Russian Orthodox. Those same "Christians" often came into Boyerker, terrorizing all of the Jews with their cries of, "Beat the Zhid!"

There were also his own unhappy memories of the Gentile kids back in New York who loved to pick on the Jews. And memories of missionaries who roamed the Jewish ghetto in New York, hoping to convert that vast Jewish population to Christ.

He thought about what his peers said concerning Jesus. They felt He was probably a colossal imposter! He was surely at the root of a lot of their problems. His name was a frequent swear word. Some men back in New York even spit on the ground when they heard the name of Jesus.

He dismissed the idea of looking back at the New Testament, but he silently acknowledged that he could *never* let this Bible out of his sight! He felt as though it were his own personal treasure!

He would steal it from the Desert Inn Hotel. (Who knows where he might find another one?) Joe pored over more of its pages that weekend. He could think of little else. Sam's nagging didn't matter, or the fact that he kept winning at the tables. Joe didn't care that they traveled all the way to Vegas to stay in a first-class hotel and then find his time spent glued to the new discovery.

Barbiturates were nearly forgotten during that time. He forgot his plan to kill Sarah and the boys.

One thing was certain: Joe Lessin had finally found at least a piece of the missing puzzle. Perhaps if he could read more of his new treasure, he could finally put that puzzle all together.

Chapter Twelve

But You Can't Be Jewish and Believe in Jesus!

Joe couldn't get Wilbur Rubottom's name out of his mind. A good customer, he had once told Joe that he and his wife were Christians. This came as no surprise, since Joe assumed that *all* Gentiles were Christians. But later Wilbur had told him that his wife was Jewish and that she now believed in Jesus!

Joe was stunned; Jews simply didn't believe in Jesus! He was alternately amused and baffled that Ann would call herself a "Hebrew Christian." Those terms seemed to be mutually exclusive—they cancelled out one another.

Maybe a simple discussion with Wilbur was warranted; he didn't want to overlook even a remote piece of the puzzle.

He'd been reading the Bible nearly five months and chose to heed the warning in Proverbs 17:1: "Better is a dry morsel, and quietness therewith, than a house full of sacrifices with strife." His house was so full of strife that he moved into a small apartment.

Joe still could work only a few hours a day because of his physical and emotional limitations. After four hours at the office each day, he turned to the Bible, drawn to it like steel to a magnet. He sensed that this book held the key to the issues of guilt and sin and death which troubled him. He felt that somehow many of the secrets to his life lay hidden somewhere in its pages.

In his study he made some startling observations. His ancestors had had an intimate relationship with God, to be sure! Two of them, in fact, Abraham and Moses, even *spoke* with God. They clearly saw God *working* in their lives. He performed miracles for His people. Many of Joe's ancient fore-bearers had heard God's voice in all sorts of ways.

So were they better Jews in those days, or had God changed? Had God stopped that kind of communication with twentieth-century man, or had He stopped communicating just with Joe Lessin?

The passage in Leviticus 16 concerning Yom Kippur, or the Day of Atonement, was very astonishing. Going through the motions of the Yom Kippur rituals was totally different from seeing it spelled out in the Bible. A glimmer of under-standing was breaking through to Joe.

He read about the two goats chosen by the High Priest; one would be God's and one would be a "scapegoat." The priest slaughtered the Lord's goat and sprinkled its blood on the mercy seat in the Holy of Holies. It bore the sins of the people on that day, and the people could vividly see that the penalty for sin was *death*. The goat, however, bore the punishment that rightfully belonged to the people. God's goat gave its life for the people; such an "exchange of life" was at the heart of the atonement concept.

Then the High Priest laid his hands upon the second goat—the scapegoat—and transferred the people's sins to it. That goat was then driven out into the wilderness, and God re-membered no more the sins against His people. A new begin-ning was possible. God saw Israel cleansed from sin and hav-ing new life!

There was the dilemma again: the barrier between God and Joe was sin! And only *God* could take it away.

But in modern times this "exchange of life" procedure had been abandoned. Since the Temple had been destroyed in 70 A.D., the sacrificial system had ceased and the Rabbis de-vised new methods by which God could be approached during Yom Kippur. And yet Joe could find no place in the Bible where God changed the Levitical concept of the "exchange of life." Nowhere did it say that mitzvahs (good deeds) would suffice; nor would fasting and praying. Apparently that had all been handed down through the Oral Law and from Jewish traditions, for it clearly was not to be found in the Bible!

God's stamp of approval didn't seem to be on the Jews' modern-day atonement procedures.

Joe was angry with himself as he headed for the Rubottom's, nearly breaking the speed limit because of his eagerness. But then maybe the most he stood to lose was a little pride, and Proverbs spoke a lot about that vice. Joe admittedly felt like a detective who had finally stumbled onto a major clue! Besides, Wilbur Rubottom never had pushed Joe about anything. Wilbur had strong convictions of his own, but he always made it clear that he would love and respect Joe no matter what he believed. But his wife's beliefs in Jesus remained a mystery to Joe.

As he entered their home late that night, he was amazed to discover that the Rubottoms had no Christian idols or statues. Jews always assumed that Christians bow and chant before such things. Perhaps this was a false stereotype; then again, maybe the Rubottoms were just different from many Christians. After all, Ann, who had once been a Jew, would hardly put up with statues and all.

Wilbur greeted Joe with his usual graciousness and warmth, and he and Ann led him to the den. Joe felt their interest and concern for him; he felt less awkward and a little more at ease. They almost seemed to anticipate his thoughts and questions, and they made every effort to make him comfortable.

"What's been happening?" Wilbur asked conversationally as they settled into their sofa and chairs for a discussion.

Joe realized there was no turning back.

"Do you remember when I went to Vegas several months ago?" he asked. "I found a Bible in the hotel room the first night. It was all very strange—that whole weekend. I heard a voice at the gambling table. I don't know if it was audible or not, but it told me to get away from the table. So I left Sam and went to our room. I was kind of shaken by the experience and wanted to write a letter or read something, but all I could find was a Gideon Bible. I read it all weekend and have hardly put it down since then. That was about five months ago."

Wilbur and Ann seemed pleased and yet in no way

pounced on Joe like hungry missionary lions.

"So I can't explain it," Joe continued. "I think I may have stumbled onto something here in this Bible, and yet I'm not so sure I can believe most of it. I mean, it has a lot of wisdom in it, but I don't know if I believe all the stories. Nor am I so sure that God has inspired it as I know you people believe."

"In all your reading," Ann asked, "have you given any thought to Jesus?"

"Ann!" Joe said rather sternly, "I'm Jewish and we just don't believe in Jesus!"

"Why not?" she asked casually. "I'm Jewish and I believe in Him."

"Then you're not a Jew!" Joe accused.

"So what am I? A Gentile?"

"Well, maybe," he replied slowly. "You're unique for sure! One of a kind!"

"Joe, a whole lot of Jewish people believe in Jesus," Ann said earnestly. "You know, Jesus was a Jew. So was the whole early church and all the writers of the New Testament. And Paul was one of the most educated Jewish scholars of his day! He was the epitome of Judaism. But in spite of his intellect, he taught an incredibly simple truth: all we need for salvation is faith in Jesus! Paul loved the Jews and was loyal to them; yet he still regarded them as lost because they wouldn't accept the truth about Jesus."

"Paul is an enigma to me I guess," Joe confessed. "And I stumble over the name of Jesus because it's in His name that so many Jewish lives have been taken."

"But we can't deny His existence," Ann said. "Even our own Jewish historians acknowledge His life and death."

"Look, I'm willing to acknowledge that Jesus may have been a good man," Joe said compromisingly; "maybe even a prophet and a fine Rabbi; but not above a whole lot of other good Jewish men. Besides, I really did come to talk about God and the Bible, not about Jesus. Even if He was who He said He was, I'm not so sure *I* could acknowledge Him. My family, you know, would be hurt. It might even kill my mother. She's not well."

Joe was sure he had made his point to the Rubottoms so they could go on to other things.

"The problem is," Wilbur said, "if we're going to talk about God, we *have* to talk about Jesus. They are one and the same."

"That's absurd!" Joe replied. Then he turned to Ann. "You know that we Jews came to establish monotheism. How can you believe this stuff? You Christians could learn some things from us Jews."

Wilbur looked up a verse in the Bible, then got up out of his chair and sat by Joe on the sofa.

"It says here," Wilbur showed him, " 'Let *us* make man in *our* image, after *our* likeness' " (Gen. 1:26). There was a brief pause.

"God is three and yet one," Wilbur went on, "and Jesus is a part of that Trinity. Like a man can be a brother, a father and a son; so God can be Father, Son and Holy Spirit."

"Okay, maybe Jesus actually believed that He was who He said He was," Joe answered reluctantly. "Maybe He was sincere and He felt that by repentance and faith He could hasten a day of peace and prosperity for all."

"Joe, do you believe that the same God who wrote the Hebrew Scriptures, the Old Testament, would allow the teachings of the New Testament to be one colossal hoax?" Wilbur asked. "Either Jesus was the long-awaited Messiah like He said He was, or He was a liar and a lunatic! And I think that a liar and even a lunatic would renounce his whole crazy hoax as those nails were about to be driven into him. But, you see, when Jesus was crucified, He was fulfilling the words of the prophet Isaiah, that He would go as a sheep to the slaughter—He wouldn't open His mouth. Isaiah and the other prophets made over three hundred messianic predictions. And unlike many "prophets" of today, *God's* prophets had to have 100% accuracy or they would be stoned! You know that."

Joe grew silent. Ann, particularly, could understand his struggle.

"No matter what people want to say about Jesus," she said quietly, "it was hard for me to ignore His lofty, yet simply stated, rabbinic teachings. I had to admit that there was something mystically beautiful about Him. He had so much mercy for mankind. He had such insight into human nature. He spoke in brilliant parables. He never seemed to do anything but good. He died for what He believed, and so did a lot of His followers. And He was so very Jewish, as were the men and women who followed Him throughout Israel!"

"Jesus was the sacrificial lamb, the paschal lamb, who was provided as an *everlasting* atonement for mankind," Wilbur added.

Here was the very problem Joe had been struggling with! Atonement, sin, Yom Kippur—the whole thing! As he listened to the Rubottoms, it sounded like *Jesus* was the one who had come to do *exactly* what was described in Leviticus!

The words of Joe's contemporaries whirled in his mind, all that they had said about Jesus. Some said that Jesus was a Jew who became a Gentile. Some said that He was a good moralist and teacher. Some said that all He accomplished was to spread Jewish ideas among the Gentiles. Others insisted that His teachings and ideas weren't His own but stolen from other Rabbis. Others insisted that he epitomized everything that was blasphemous to a Jew! The only thing all of them agreed upon was that Jesus was *not* the Messiah He claimed to be.

"I'll say it again," Joe said stubbornly. "You *can't* believe in Jesus and remain a Jew!"

"Joe," Wilbur replied, "if a Negro becomes a Buddhist, he is still a Negro. It makes no difference what you *believe*; you still remain what you are born. Whether you're an Orthodox Jew or an atheist, you're still a Jew. You're a descendant of Abraham, and *nothing* can change that."

Joe knew he should walk out on this whole conversation, but for some reason he couldn't. As confusing and offensive as it was becoming, he knew he had to stay and hear these people out. *Something* had worked for Wilbur and Ann Rubottom. They were at peace with each other and with themselves. And they surely seemed to have peace with God. Wilbur had carefully examined what he believed. He didn't necessarily accept things because someone told him to do so. He studied a situation and often drew his own conclusions. He was so sure now about what he believed concerning God and Jesus, obviously having no doubt whatsoever.

"Our concept of the Messiah," Joe said, "is that He will usher in a time of peace. So where's the peace Jesus brought?" He sat back more comfortably now, confident that he had raised a valid objection to Jesus' messiahship.

"How could He bring peace when He was rejected?" Ann asked. "Besides, His *first* coming was for the purpose of suffering and dying for the sins of the world. The Bible says that 'without the shedding of blood there is no remission of sins.' [1] Jesus came the first time to shed His blood and atone for the sins of mankind. Then anybody who believes on His name will be saved from those sins, and they will have eternal life."

Joe reflected back on that Yom Kippur service in New York. It was man's hopelessness that drove him to despair that day—hopelessness because there was no sin-bearer to atone for the wretched sins of which man was capable. His despair was because of the frantic circle without end, always coming back to the same dismal conclusion: there is no way to be *certain* about life after death because there is no adequate sin-bearer for men's sins. All men are doomed.

But now the Bible and the Rubottoms were claiming that this blasphemous Jewish zealot, Jesus, was the answer to both of those dilemmas! Only because he'd never had a satisfactory answer to that problem was he inclined to stay put and hear them out.

"Consider what your own prophets said about the coming Messiah," Wilbur said. "Look how Jesus' credentials meet those specifications.

"Micah said that the Messiah would be born in Bethlehem[2]; Isaiah said He would be born of a virgin[3]; Isaiah also said He would minister to the Gentiles[4]; Isaiah said His suffering would bring salvation[5]; Zechariah said He would enter

---

1. Hebrews 9:22
2. Mic. 5:2
3. Isa. 7:14

4. Isa. 42:1; 49:1-8
5. Isa. 52:13-53:12

Jerusalem on a donkey[1]; and that He would be forsaken by His disciples.[2] The entire crucifixion experience is talked about in Psalm 22. The Psalmist also says that the Messiah will be forsaken by a friend[3] and that He would be a descendant of David.[4] These prophecies, plus more than three hundred others, are *perfectly* fulfilled by Jesus."

"It could be coincidence," Joe said skeptically.

"Do you have any idea what the chances for that are?" Ann asked. "I think it would be off the board!"

"Then maybe Jesus planned it all—you know, sort of plotted His messiahship." Couldn't *something* Joe suggested break this whole theory wide open?

"How could Jesus plot the fact that He was to be born in Bethlehem!" Ann tried to reason. "Or plot the *time* of His coming, the *manner* of His birth, His betrayal, and the price of His betrayal, the *manner* of His death, the casting of lots for His clothes and the dozen of other *specific* prophecies about Him? Besides, not even a liar or a lunatic would plot to get himself crucified! That whole crucifixion account was written by our prophets centuries before crucifixion had been invented by the Romans. I think God went to a whole lot of trouble to make sure that Jesus had *all* the right credentials to be the Messiah!"

"The name of Jesus has been used to scorch Jewish homes and bodies," Joe said angrily. "The cross has been a symbol of death to us. Even you can't deny that, Ann! Jesus and His Christian followers have been our number-one enemy."

"If Jesus had been here in person," Ann said, "He never would have sanctioned such acts. The words Gentile and Christian are not synonymous. A lot of people call themselves Christian, and neither their attitudes nor their behavior are very Christlike, which is what it means to be a Christian. The New Testament teaches us that 'salvation is of the Jews,' and it forbids their persecution. A lot of people call themselves

---

1. Zech. 9:9   3. Ps. 41:9
2. Zech. 13:7   4. Ps. 132:11

'Christian' when they aren't; they use the name of Jesus for their own war against the Jews. But a *true* Christian has Christ dwelling within him and therefore wants to do nothing less than what Jesus would do—love all men."

"Jesus' death is the only method of redemption, the only way we have the assurance that our names are written in heaven—and not just for one more year as with Yom Kippur," Wilbur added. "With Jesus, forgiveness is freely offered to all who will accept it. When Jesus said on the cross, 'It is finished,' He meant that He had taken on Him the sin of the world. His job was finished. Sin was finished. Death was conquered for everyone who would believe on the name of Jesus. A holy and a righteous God had poured out His wrath on His Son, Jesus, so that God could justly forgive the rest of humanity in love."

Joe got up and paced the floor for a few moments without speaking. Finally Wilbur interrupted the silence.

"You have told me there are two things which have haunted you: death and eternity. Jesus offers an answer, because He came to forgive sin so that we all might have eternal life. The Bible says that 'all have sinned and fallen short of the glory of God,' [1] and that the 'wages of sin is death,' [2] but that 'God demonstrated his own love towards us, in that while we were yet sinners, Christ died for us.' [3] There is no other way to God and to eternal life except one believes on Jesus, confesses his sins and asks Christ into his life to make him a new creature. *Then* Jesus can begin to restore your health, Joe, and your business and your family. Can you really think of any reason why you shouldn't give Him your life today?"

Joe could think of a hundred excuses.

"I just can't do it now," he said weakly, turning to leave.

"How about taking a couple books along with you?" Wilbur encouraged him. "I want you to read them and then give

---

1. Rom. 3:23
2. Rom. 6:23
3. Rom. 5:8

us a call so we can talk some more. The books deal with a lot of the questions you're asking. Some deal with the Jewishness of Jesus, and they talk about other Jews who have believed in Jesus—men like yourself, Joe. Will you take them?"

"Sure," Joe shrugged. Why not? If this was, indeed, all a part of the mystery, he felt he shouldn't overlook anything.

"Joe, just answer me this question," Wilbur said as he and Ann walked him to the front door. "Would you rather have Jesus and have eternal life, or would you rather keep going your own way in life?"

"Right now I don't know, Wilbur. I really don't know. I'll call you soon when I can sort through my thoughts."

Chapter Thirteen

A Redeemer Discovered

For one week Joe could hardly put aside his reading. One of his previous observations was that the Bible was always prophetically accurate. What the Jewish prophets had predicted for Israel centuries ago had come true. And what some of them predicted for future generations—perhaps even Joe's generation—were also coming to pass.

Nothing spoke more loudly to him than the rebirth of the State of Israel! Fresh in his mind, it had occurred just a few years earlier; but at the time he knew nothing about Bible prophecy and fulfillment.

Joe reflected back to that spring day in 1948. The celebration in the Jewish community had been greater than when either of the two World Wars ended. When Israel became a nation in May, 1948, every latent streak of Zionism within the hearts of Jewish people everywhere was aroused. They danced in the streets of every major city, proclaiming, "Next year in Jerusalem!" A thousand Jewish weddings in one place could not equal the joyous spirit of that day in May.

Joe couldn't deny that many of the prophets in the Bible had said that God would bring the Jewish people back to their land again. And once they were back, according to the Bible, they would never again be uprooted from their land. That sounded delightful to Joe, whose people had been in exile for forty centuries! It was one of the biblical facts Joe regretted having missed earlier, for such concepts spoke of *hope* in a better day ahead for the Jews.

But present reality brought Joe little personal hope. Family problems worsened and Don began to show signs of the same hostility, fear and anger that Joe had had at the same age. He recalled Don's Bar Mitzvah nearly two years earlier.

His rigid face had shown no expression that day when he threw his prayer shawl and his yarmulke into the car.

"I've done what I'm supposed to do and now I'm finished!" Don had stated that day. "I want nothing more to do with this."

It appeared that the family turmoil had left its deepest mark on Don. He resented Joe and seldom spoke when he came around. Don then took out his hurts on his mother, hurling verbal abuse at her daily. Don's grades tumbled to barely passing. He delighted in taking out further hostilities, too, on his younger brother, Roy. More than once Joe found Roy nursing wounds inflicted on him by his older brother.

Such rebellion and anger surely were leading Don into serious trouble. And what made Joe even more fearful was that Roy would follow in his older brother's footsteps, since Don was the predominate male figure in his young life.

Could Jesus really solve these problems? Those words sounded so foreign to Joe's Jewish mind. It was much easier to bury the hurts and fears by increased dosages of barbiturates.

Besides, Jesus would complicate his life too much. Joe figured he would certainly lose more than he would gain. His family would turn against him completely if Jesus came into the picture. And the family structure was the most important thing to a Jew. The strength that safeguards life and survival rests in the home. The family, God and Israel were the future of Judaism; all would be seriously endangered if the family were shattered. Divorces were few, and children generally were raised successfully so that family members could take pride in them and their accomplishments.

And yet here was Jesus saying that *He* had to come before everything and everyone—even before parents and children. Jesus asked a lot from His followers!

But Joe couldn't dismiss that whole conversation with the Rubottoms regarding atonement. He couldn't ignore the fact that Jesus was presented in the New Testament as the *final, lasting* atonement for mankind. Every Jew, religious or not, knew the importance of a blood atonement.

Adam and Eve's first coverings were animal skins. The

nakedness that sin had revealed needed to be covered. But the blood of several animals was shed to provide the covering.

The great men of Jewish history—Abraham, Isaac, Jacob—approached God by means of blood sacrifices.

The redemptive element of blood ran through the entire Law given on Mt. Sinai—all 613 commandments. The words of Moses particularly impressed Joe when he read Leviticus 17:11: "For the life of the flesh is in the blood: and I have given it to you upon the altar to make an atonement for your souls: for it is the blood that makes atonement by reason of the life."

Joe knew that when God's commandments were disobeyed in the Bible, the means of atonement for the sin was a blood sacrifice. The Temple in Jerusalem was built to expedite the required shedding of blood for the atonement of the people's sins. The Holy of Holies could be entered only once a year on Yom Kippur by the High Priest who carried the blood sacrifice. He then sprinkled the blood on the ark of the covenant.

But the sacrificial system became a burden to many Jews in Bible times. Out of convenience, many of them built their *own* sacrificial altars nearer their homes, rather than travel to Jerusalem. God's prophets, however, considered this a deviation from the Law.

Then came Isaiah: He said that the burden of sacrifice would forever be lifted by a suffering servant: Joe now realized that this could point to Jesus; the Messiah was to provide the blood sacrifice for sin once and for all. If so, all a person needed to do was to accept Jesus' death on his behalf and his sin would be forgiven. The Messiah's blood could very well be the means of redemption now.

Clearly there had been no method of blood sacrifice since the Temple was destroyed in 70 A.D. And only the sacrifices offered there were acceptable to God. A new Temple had never been erected. So surely God must have provided *another* means of atonement in light of that! And if it was Jesus, the so-called Messiah, why hadn't the Jews been told? Why didn't they believe it? Why was there such universal rejection of Jesus by the Jews?

" 'Believe on the name of the Lord Jesus and you shall be

saved,' " Wilbur had said to Joe on a few occasions, and he couldn't shake it from his mind. It sounded so utterly simple, and yet so complicated in light of his family's predicted reaction!

Joe pored over his reading material at his desk that hot Memorial Day in 1951. Suddenly a sharp, prolonged pain stabbed him, first under his left arm and then across his chest. He recognized the familiar pain from his heart attack of some years back. But this time, every ounce of strength was sapped from him. Trying to reach for the telephone just inches away, he could barely lift the receiver off the hook. And yet his breathing was normal. If, in fact, this was another heart attack, he knew he should be dead, for the pain was many times worse than with the previous attack. Only a concentrated effort enabled him to dial Dr. David Weiss, his doctor for some time. The telephone felt as if it weighed twenty pounds in his hands. After dialing, Joe was so exhausted he felt like he had just run a marathon.

"Can you get to your bed?" Dr. Weiss inquired.

"I don't know. The pain has drained my strength."

"Try to lie down," Dr. Weiss suggested. "Don't move until I get to your apartment. Try to relax."

Joe cautiously got up from his desk and rubbed his chest as he inched toward the bed. He carried his Bible with him, though it felt like a granite block in his hand. Setting it on the table next to the bed, Joe lay back and stared at the ceiling. Motion or mental exertion seemed to increase his pain. He concentrated on the ticking of the clock beside him.

Dr. Weiss didn't bother to knock when he arrived some time later. But as he approached Joe, his serious countenance abruptly turned to curiosity as he spotted the Bible on the table.

"Who's the religious one in the family?" he asked, amused. It seemed strange that his first question had nothing to do with Joe's current physical condition!

"I guess I am," Joe replied.

"So tell me, what's in that book?" the doctor asked quizzically as he sat on the edge of the bed.

"It contains a lot of answers to life's problems," Joe replied. "I stole it about six months ago from the Desert Inn in Vegas. I was at a desperately low point in my life. You remember how depressed I was about that time, don't you? I thought about murdering Sarah and the boys, then killing myself."

Dr. Weiss nodded.

"But when I found this Bible," Joe continued with more enthusiasm and strength, "I started to read it because I sensed it might have some answers for my miserable condition. Now I can hardly set it aside."

"And what has it told you? How has it solved your problems?"

"Well, I don't know if it has solved too much, but that is because I haven't allowed it to. But it's full of wisdom, and the history of the Jews, and it has a lot to say about a coming Messiah."

Dr. Weiss remained silent for a moment.

"Those books on my desk," Joe said, "tell me that *Jesus* is the long-awaited Messiah of our people. He is the suffering servant spoken of in Isaiah 53. Let me read it to you out of the Bible."

Dr. Weiss handed Joe the book and waited with interest as he searched for the passage.

" 'Yet it pleased the Lord to bruise him: he hath put him to grief: when thou shalt make his soul an offering for sin, he shall see his seed, he shall prolong his days, and the pleasure of the Lord shall prosper in his hand. He shall see the travail of his soul, and shall be satisfied: by his knowledge shall my righteous servant justify many: for he shall bear their iniquities' [Isa. 53:10-11].

"Some years ago," Joe continued, "I dashed out of my last Yom Kippur service back in the Bronx. I left because I saw the hopelessness of our people—of all mankind, in fact. No one had hope because no one could properly atone for sins so terrible that God said we should die by being stoned, burned, beheaded or strangled. I sat on a park bench in despair because it was true! Humanity is in such a mess that unless something or someone can atone for our wretchedness, all is futile. I know we need a sin-bearer; fasting, praying and beating the chest on Yom Kippur simply isn't enough to satisfy God."

"So what is?" Dr. Weiss inquired. His own Jewish background had obviously left him as well with few answers.

"As I read the Bible, I see that the only thing that satisfies God is shed blood. God knew that the Temple in Jerusalem would be destroyed as it finally was in 70 A.D. So God planned to have *another* method of atonement ready, and that was the shed blood of Jesus, the Messiah, spoken of here in Isaiah 53. His shed blood on the cross would forever pay for the sins of our people and for all mankind. Animal blood would never be necessary again."

Dr. Weiss got up and went to the telephone.

"I'm going to call my wife and cancel our dinner engagement," he said. "She will be upset with me because it's an important date with friends. But I want to hear more of this."

When he finished his conversation with his wife, he then called his office and notified them that he was completely unavailable for the rest of the evening.

"I'm on an extremely important case," he told his answering service. "I'm not to be interrupted tonight for any reason," he said with finality.

Joe was amused, for so far he hadn't even asked him how the pain was!

"My wife and I are in a conflict," Dr. Weiss said as he returned to the edge of the bed. "She is a Gentile and she wants our two children to be brought up in a Christian church somewhere. I want them to have proper Jewish training. But I'm open to the other if it makes sense."

"Christianity *is* Jewish," Joe stated.

"How come?"

"Because Jesus is a Jew and so were all of His followers. He was born in a Jewish town—Bethlehem—just like our prophet Micah had predicted. The early church was a Hebrew Christian experience, and all the writers of the Bible, Old and New Testament, were Jewish men. The Bible says that Jesus was sent only to the lost sheep of the house of Israel. By and large, they rejected Him. Then the gospel was made available to the Gentiles. As I see it, the Gentiles could be considered proselytes to biblical Judaism. They accept the Jewish Messiah, the Jewish Bible and the Jewish blood atonement. The early church was made up of Jews who believed in Messiah Jesus. Then so many Gentiles came to believe in Jesus that it came to be thought of as a *Gentile* religion! But the Messiah was promised to the Jewish people first."

"Are you saying, then, that one can be a Christian and yet remain Jewish?"

"Yes, I am." Joe was amazed with the thought that he really believed that!

"So we still have war," Dr. Weiss said skeptically. "Where is the *peace* that this Jesus is to usher in?"

"I think that if our people would have accepted Jesus, that He would have brought about the kingdom of peace. But our people rejected Him. They chose, in fact, to free another prisoner and crucify Jesus instead. He was given no witnesses and He was tried at night, which was illegal. But the Bible speaks about a peace of the *heart*—a peace that passes all understanding. Then, even if the world is at war, those who believe in the Messiah can have peace of mind and peace with each other."

"I still can't forgive God, or the Gentiles, for allowing the slaughter of six million innocent people. Why should I align myself with either of them when they stood silently watching that?"

"It's not a matter of aligning yourself with *Gentiles*, because not all Gentiles are Christians. Some of them masquerade as Christians, like they did in Russia when they forced Jews to convert to Christianity and be baptized. They may have had religion, but they weren't *Christians*. Besides, if the Czars had had their way—and Hitler and Haman and Pharaoh, too—there would be none of us left alive! God *must* have intervened and spared a good many of us, while a whole host of other nations who have come against our people have disappeared."

"So how do you figure that Jesus is the Messiah?" Dr.

Weiss asked in an attempt to get to the heart of the issue. "What gives Him the right to make such a claim? Why couldn't He be a fraud?"

"Because He was described over three hundred times in the Bible and He fit the necessary description of the Messiah *perfectly*." Joe realized he was using some of the very words that the Rubottoms had used. He reached for the list of messianic prophecies found in the Old Testament. He kept such a list in the back of his Bible for easy reference, since the night he talked with Wilbur and Ann. Then Joe sat up in bed, next to Dr. Weiss, and pointed out some of the messianic prophecies.

"Here are some of those three hundred specifications that the Messiah had to fill. In this column is the Old Testament description, and in this column is the New Testament fulfillment, showing Jesus as that perfect fulfillment."

They looked up two dozen such verses. Dr. Weiss was not argumentative or defensive, rather, sitting quietly and considering each verse.

"The Messiah had to fulfill these specifications *perfectly*," Joe reminded him. "There was no room for error on the part of God's prophets. You can see how Jesus fits the credentials to a T. If Jesus had missed just *one* specification, He wouldn't be the Messiah. But He didn't miss one! God's batting average has to be one thousand! His hall of fame players of Old Testament days couldn't bat just three hundred!"

Dr. Weiss wanted more proof, so they looked up another two dozen such passages as Joe struggled to find them in the Bible.

An hour later, Joe stated the matter as simply as he could.

"The only hope for mankind is in this book," he said. "And believing on the name of Jesus is the only way to peace and life and the only assurance of life after death."

Dr. Weiss finally stood to leave.

"This has been helpful," he stated. "I will give serious thought to the things we have talked about tonight."

Joe walked him to the door; as he closed it and heard the doctor's footsteps go down the hall, he realized that Dr. Weiss had not asked him how he felt, asked no questions about the stabbing pain, prescribed no medication, nor given advice or words of warning about his heart condition! Just as interesting was the fact that every bit of pain and discomfort had left the moment the doctor walked into his room earlier that evening.

It appeared to Joe's limited understanding of the ways of God that God had arranged the meeting just so Joe could talk to the doctor about Jesus, God and the Bible.

Now could God really convince *Joe* of the truth of all that had been shared that evening?

He returned to his desk with his Bible in hand. Why did he feel that the puzzle wasn't all together quite yet? He thumbed through the Bible and reflected on the evening with Dr. Weiss. Joe had preached Jesus to him for nearly three hours that night. So why couldn't Joe just accept it all by faith and yield his life to God? Maybe it was too big a step to have even a shred of doubt! Hadn't Wilbur said at one time that the Jew requires a sign? Maybe he should ask for a sign! Something to show him, without a doubt, that Jesus is the true Messiah of Israel and the world.

He opened the Bible to Isaiah again and pored over its pages. This time Isaiah 9:6 jumped out to him: "For unto us a child is born, unto us a son is given: and the government shall be upon his shoulder: and his name shall be called Wonderful, Counsellor, The mighty God, The everlasting Father, *The Prince of Peace.*"

How is this possible? He had seen "The Prince of Peace" on dozens of Christmas cards, clearly referring to the Gentile God, Jesus. So what is this doing in the Old Testament? Joe's stiff-necked skepticism wanted to cancel out everything he had said to Dr. Weiss moments earlier!

He read on, hoping for an answer to the dilemma that loomed larger in his mind than it needed to. But if Joe Lessin was going to commit his life to Jesus, he had to be *sure* of *everything* he believed: He couldn't risk the loss of every loved one if he might be pinning his hopes and ideas on a phony Messiah!

His heart leaped as he came upon Isaiah 11:10: "And in

that day there shall be a root of Jesse, which shall stand for an ensign of the people; *to it shall the Gentiles seek....* "

That was it! That was how the Prince of Peace and the Gentiles could be reconciled. That was his answer and his sign. At precisely 11:00 p.m. he finished Isaiah 11 and clearly saw that Jesus was, indeed, the Messiah of Israel—*whom the Gentiles shall seek,* but who came first to the Jews!

Jesus was all that He said He was. And He was the sin-bearer for which Joe had anguished for so many years. Everything he had talked about to Dr. Weiss that night was true. Jesus' shed blood on the cross was the *only* atonement anybody needed. If His shed blood was applied to the doorposts of his heart, he would forever be saved from his sins!

Joe got down on his knees beside his bed, in an awkward attempt to do what needed to be done. His prayer was not eloquent, but God knew the sincerity of his heart at the moment.

"God, I believe that Jesus is the Messiah of our people," he prayed.

He remained on his knees for many minutes as he waited for something to happen. Should bells ring? Should there be a flash of light? He didn't know. His legs began to ache as he remained on his knees, waiting for God's voice but hearing only traffic sounds and a radio from the next apartment.

Finally he arose and paced the room. Something was missing. If there was a "limbo-state" of Christianity, he felt locked into it. What had gone wrong? What had he forgotten?

He knelt again.

"God, *you* know why I'm feeling this way. *Show me* what it is I should be doing."

He waited for many moments, listening for some still, small voice.

Sin! Of course! Joe had failed to confess his sin to God and tell God that he was a sinner, lost and in need of a Savior—Jesus. That was what had been overlooked! All that had to be confessed to God.

Afterward the burden was lifted! For the first time in his life, he had *freedom* from the bondages of depression, doubt and fear. He had never come close to this kind of *total* freedom before—no matter how much he had prayed or fasted, kept kosher or followed a dozen other suggestions that friends, relatives, Rabbis and others had prescribed for his pitiful condition. It was sin that had been the constant weight that never eased its burden on him. Just as heavy had been the fear of death.

But at last the perpetual burden of sin, judgment and condemnation was lifted! Lifted because finally he had recognized Jesus as his sin-bearer—the atonement God had provided for him and for everyone who would believe in Him and be saved.

The search had finally ended. The pieces finally fit properly together.

But the real journey had just begun.

Second only to the new inner peace and assurance he felt was the incredible new love he felt for his parents, for Sarah and for his sons. They, too, had to have this new kind of assurance and peace as well—especially his sons, who would surely follow in Joe's own footsteps of despair unless they found Jesus in time.

It was just as well that God kept the road through the next ten years shrouded in mystery. Otherwise he would have despaired again in a new way.

Chapter Fourteen
All Things New

Joe would never forget the look on Dr. Weiss' face when he saw that Joe's heart condition had completely disappeared. There wasn't even a scar on his heart. The doctor's testing procedures were rigorous and thorough. He double-checked some tests to make sure he hadn't overlooked something. Yet every test turned out negative. Joe Lessin's heart was totally repaired and he had begun to gain weight and strength. It was a tremendous testimonial to Dr. Weiss, giving further credibility to all that Joe had shared with him that night.

But the barbiturates and the sleeping pills were no longer merely a crutch—they were a way of life. He needed them, physically and emotionally. And yet if Joe was going to turn his life totally over to Jesus, he had to turn his health over to Him, too. He had to trust Jesus for the unknowns and he had to trust Him with the difficult areas he sensed would develop.

A persistent voice awakened him early one morning. In that pre-dawn muddled state of mind, the voice seemed to be telling him to clean out his medicine cabinet. In that strange command, Joe could sense the assurance of God. He felt that God wanted him to rid the medicine cabinet of *all* its contents.

The thing that impressed him the most was the *completeness* of the command. He realized that trusting Jesus meant trusting Him instead of aspirin and antacids as well as barbiturates and sleeping pills. Not that aspirin and antacids were wrong for everybody else; it was just that God wanted Joe Lessin to see that He was to be Joe's total sufficiency! God wanted to show him that He was greater than any problem and greater than any man-made solution!

Joe could do nothing but obey that still, small voice. He dumped everything down the drain, thereby allowing God to be his great Physician. Time would show that he would never have to touch those medications again, though temptation often came. What a confirmation that Jesus was, indeed, making all things new in his life!

Joe felt the urgency to get back with Sarah and the boys and restore them as a family before it was too late. But this was no easy assignment. Joe was prepared to experience misunderstanding, but not total rejection.

Joe had spent days preparing himself as much as he could to meet his family and break the news to them. He asked God to seal his mouth shut should he want to speak to them impatiently. He was aware of Jesus' words in Matthew 11: "For I am come to set a man at variance with his father, and the daughter against her mother." Not deliberately, of course, but because they might not understand one another and thus Jesus would come between them.

Jesus also said, "He that loveth father or mother, son or daughter, more than me, is not worthy of me."

Joe was aware that Jesus seemed to ask a lot from His followers; yet throughout history men and women were willing to obey Him—all the way to the burning stakes and the arenas filled with hungry lions. That possibly would be easier, however, than telling his family that he now believed in Jesus.

He had approached Sarah timidly early one Saturday morning. Now as he walked up her front stairs he felt more jittery than when he first courted her! He followed her around the house, engaged in small talk and discussion about the boys. He couldn't seem to get to the point.

"Could we sit down and talk a minute?" he finally asked nervously.

Sarah looked skeptical. She had seen Joe in enough difficulties to conclude that he might be on the downward slide again. In the past, such "serious" conversations generally turned into morbid talks about death and the hopelessness of the human race.

"What are you depressed about now?" Sarah asked, humoring him as she anticipated the usual trend of conversation.

"I'm not depressed, Sarah. That's what I want to talk to you about. Something has happened to me."

She seemed almost startled. It was no small accomplishment for Joe Lessin to change for the *better*. They both pulled out a chair at the kitchen table and sat down.

"So tell me, what is it this time?" she asked cautiously.

"It's God. I've finally found Him," Joe took a deep breath, "and I found Him in Jesus."

Sarah shook her head. "You certainly go from one extreme to another," she said, perplexed. "But did you have to go *that* far? Do you know what this will do to your parents?"

"I know. But I had to do it." Joe rushed on. "Remember when I went to Vegas last year with Sam? I found a Bible in our hotel room and I couldn't stop reading it. It captivated me for months. Since then, it's been like some invisible hand pulling me towards Jesus. I fought the urge, then I tried to ignore it, but it never went away. So I studied the Bible more closely and read other books. When I shared my discovery with Dr. Weiss one night, I realized that I believed most of what I had told him! But I needed just one more piece to tie it all together and I received it that same night. God convinced me that Jesus was exactly who He said He was: the Messiah of our people."

"If it works for you, Joe, it's all right. But I don't need it. And I don't think you should even tell your parents."

"Sarah, I want to come home again. I want us to be a family like we used to be back in New York."

"You can come home," she said, "but you can't bring Jesus into this house. You can even go to the Gentile's church, but I want you to be quiet about Jesus around here. Those are my only conditions."

Joe's heart sank. How could he possibly keep quiet about this new walk with Jesus? How could he bottle it up inside of himself and pretend that he could turn it off when around the house? It would never work.

"Well, maybe we could go out now and then," he offered as an alternative. "You know, we could go out on a date a few times a week like we used to." Maybe if he spent enough time with Sarah, he thought, he could slowly win her to himself and to Jesus.

Sarah was agreeable. She was still hesitant about his talking to Don and Roy about Christ, however. But she was willing to try to make things work. They would both try a little harder if he wouldn't push Jesus too much.

Joe determined to show her and the boys all the love of the Lord that he could.

Wilbur and Ann Rubottom were a continual source of encouragement and help.

"Jesus asks that we forsake everyone, if necessary," Ann reminded him, "and follow Him. We're to take up our cross and go where He leads. Nothing and no one can come before Him. We may not even like where it is He's leading us, but He promises never to leave us or forsake us."

"Look how many years it took for your heart of stone to be made flesh," Wilbur exhorted. "Now you want your loved ones to embrace these same new beliefs overnight. It may take years, Joe; the proof of what you have done will be evidenced through your changed life. What you say must stack up with how you live. You may have to earn some credibility in their eyes! You need to remind yourself of all the stereotypes *you* once believed, because you can be sure that your family believes them, too!"

Faith was obviously a strong basis for the Christian walk. Faith that God could save his family was difficult at this point.

"It's not just trusting God for *your* life," Wilbur said. "It's trusting Him, by faith, for every person you care for. It is your faith that pleases God the most—particularly in the difficult areas of your life, like with loved ones. Your job is to love your family, to pray for them, and to put them into God's hands. Don't ever forget, though, about the secret weapon we Christians have: prayer! Few people can outrun those prayers offered by God's people!"

Sarah was relatively tolerant of Joe's new religious views; his parents were another story. Eliezer could unleash his fear-

ful violence on him; Golda's health could take a terrible turn
for the worse.

Joe put off the difficult assignment for weeks. And yet how
could he forgive himself if something happened to his parents
and he had withheld this news from them? He was afraid word
would get back to Pa and Ma before *he* got to them, so he kept
his Bible hidden under his coat when he went out. That was
no way to live and, besides, it wasn't honoring to God to hide
Him and His Word away. If Joe denied His Lord, Jesus might
do the same to him, according to the Bible.

He prayed for days for the right approach. He enlisted the
prayers of a dozen other Christians that he met through Wilbur and Ann. Fortified with confidence, he finally made prep-
arations to tell them a week later; but by the time his feet hit
their front steps, his legs felt like jello. *Never* would an assignment be as difficult as this one! It seemed to Joe a tremendous
paradox: he loved his parents so much that he had to tell them
news that would hurt them beyond measure.

He sat awkwardly with them in the living room. This time
Joe wasted no time. Why prolong the agony?

"I believe, Pa and Mama, that Jesus is the Messiah of our
people."

The response was almost predictable. Pa put his coffee cup
down without spilling a drop, but his face was distorted with
anger. That simple sentence had just shattered his world. He
had had much disappointment in his life, but this was the last
straw.

Golda broke into tears; for several moments, no one said a
word.

"Pa, please try to understand," Joe began.

"There is *nothing* to understand," he said walking toward
the front door. "You are no longer my son. Get out." He had
not raised his voice but his face was red.

"Pa, let me explain!"

"Yusef, how could you do this?" Golda wailed. "Now you
are a goy! You have joined the side of our enemies!"

Pa stood at the front door, holding it open for Joe.

"You will no longer be mentioned in our home," Pa said.

"Don't you remember that awful depression and fear I've always had?" Joe protested, still not ready to give up and leave. "It's gone. God has taken it all away. He's also taken away my need for all the pills and He has healed my heart! Doesn't that say something to you?"

"Yusef, you must see a psychiatrist," Golda pleaded. "You're not well. This is just temporary," she appealed desperately to Pa. "You tell Yusef he needs to see a psychiatrist. This is a passing thing. He will get over it. This new belief gives him relief from all the pressure he has gone through. You tell him, Eliezer, to see a good doctor again. You go back to that good Dr. Weiss. You make him give you some medicine so you can get well again."

"Mama, I don't need any of that," Joe insisted.

"So you go to the Gentile church now, is that right?" Golda asked, trying to wipe away the tears.

"Mama, Jesus doesn't belong only to the Gentiles. He came to our people first and we rejected Him like some of our prophets predicted."

"You come here on Sunday, Yusef," she begged. "Just don't talk about this anymore; come back on Sunday."

Pa finally closed the front door in disgust and left the living room.

"Mama, don't you remember how long I've looked for answers to death and eternity and all? Well, I finally—"

She wouldn't let him finish. "Have you been baptized?" Golda asked; then held her breath. Her mind flashed back to the forced conversions and baptisms in Russia. She had witnessed such things.

"Yes, Mama, I've been baptized."

Golda broke down again and hid her face in her hands. The seal of finality in the eyes of any Jew was Christian baptism, and Joe knew it.

Finally Pa stormed back into the room. "This is killing your mother!" he raged. "This time I mean it. Get out of this house. You are a traitor to our people!"

"Pa!" Joe protested. "You allow a communist or an atheist in your house and you don't call *them* traitors!"

"You were sick, broke and depressed," Pa said with finality, "so you turned to this Gentile God for a crutch."

"Yes, you're right," Joe said as he rose to leave. "I was lost, miserable and undone, too. But now I am well."

"You make us pay for your mental instability," Pa said. "Leave immediately."

"I am a changed person, but I am still a Jew," Joe said in conclusion as he moved toward the door. "I love you both very much. Always remember that I love you both, Pa and Mama, no matter what happens and no matter what you think of me."

Golda's crying could be heard even as he closed the front gate and walked down the street.

Chapter Fifteen

One of "Us" or One of "Them"

Don and Roy were unusually uncomfortable in their dad's apartment that night. Joe remembered his own fear of his dad when he was their age. He welcomed most any excuse so he wouldn't have to be with his dad, even if it meant renting his own peddler's wagon so they could go their separate ways.

And now a generation later, it was clear that his emotional problems had affected his own sons even more.

No one in his family appreciated the fact that he had found a remedy for all his problems. Finally he had found some answers, had acquired peace and purpose to life; yet because the Gentile God, Jesus, was a part of that solution, it appeared his family would rather that Joe be sick and depressed.

Whether Sarah approved or not, he had to speak to his sons about the Lord. Sarah probably had little real understanding of Christianity, and the story might get confused. Joe's suspicion had been reinforced a week earlier when Don called him a Catholic. Since there were only *two* kinds of people in their eyes—Jews and Gentiles—all believers in Jesus must be Catholics. That stereotype was enhanced because of the Mexican-Catholic neighborhood where they lived. All that most Jewish people knew about Catholics was that they used a lot of "idols"; therefore, they must be rather pagan.

There was no middle ground to a Jew; you were either one of "us" or one of "them."

Joe painfully realized what an outcast he'd become to the family. He was an exile at the least and a traitor and a dirty word at the worst. Now Don and Roy felt that they had been further "abandoned" by their dad, and the built-in resentment for him was not easily broken down.

The three of them sat around Joe's tiny kitchen table eating spaghetti. Don pushed his food around, nervous and irritated over the occasion. He had reluctantly consented to see his dad only out of obligation.

And Roy generally took his cues from Don. In spite of the verbal and physical abuse he received from his older brother, Roy still found his source of security in Don.

"I wanted you boys to come over here for a specific reason," Joe said, dishing up some more spaghetti for Roy. "I know I'm not very popular in your eyes. I walked out on you and your mother because I was a sick man. You don't know how much I regret it. And I still love all of you. But I found something—maybe I should say, Someone—who has touched my life in a marvelous way."

Don pushed his plate away, obviously disliking this whole event—particularly the turn in the conversation.

"If you mean Jesus," he scowled, "Roy and I aren't interested. You're the goy in the family. One is already too many."

"Son, you may not like that I'm a Christian, but you're not the world's best Jew, you know. I remember the day you gave it all up on your Bar Mitzvah two years ago. So now how come you're so Jewish? I think you're just reacting to all the bad press our family feeds you about me."

"You've hurt everyone in the family," Don replied heatedly. "I resent that just like I resent that Christian stuff you have on the car radio. We all know what you're trying to do. You're trying to make me and Roy convert and become Gentiles like you did."

Roy looked bewildered. At eleven he was still young enough to be persuaded in either direction.

"Boys, I made a lot of mistakes. I treated you and your ma very poorly. I was a miserable, undone man and I wallowed in every misery I could think of. I thought a lot about suicide, so you've got to know how serious my depression was. And I made you guys and your ma pay for it. But then Jesus touched me one night quite recently. Not only did He heal me, He also gave me a new love for you and for Sarah. And for my parents, too, and you know how afraid I was of my dad. But all of those feelings—the fear, anger, hopelessness—left me the night I gave my life to Jesus."

"Let Roy and me work things out for ourselves, okay?" Don said sarcastically.

"Not if that means being cruel to your mother," Joe insisted. "You yell and scream at her and you beat up your kid brother here."

Don's body stiffened once more. "Leave us alone!" he insisted through clenched teeth. "Convert the Gentiles if you want, but leave your family alone!"

Joe turned to Roy. "Son, what do they say in Hebrew School about Jesus?"

"They say He was a Rabbi, and probably a good man," Roy replied. "But the Gentiles adopted Him as their God, and we Jews don't have anything to do with Jesus."

"Do you believe that, Roy?"

"I believe it because I'm supposed to believe it and because Don tells me to."

"Do they tell you in Hebrew School, Roy, that a Messiah is coming someday to save our people?"

"Sure, Dad."

"But they don't tell you that Jesus is that Messiah. That He came to our people two thousand years ago to save us all from our sins."

"Roy, we're getting out of here," Don said, pushing his chair out to leave.

"No, you're not!" Joe commanded. "I'm still your father and you will do as I say."

Don glared at the floor rather than look Joe in the face.

"I am called a Christ-killer sometimes at school," Roy said. "When we sing Christmas carols in school, I leave out the word 'Jesus' or 'Christ.' "

"Boys, I want to say to you that I'm sorry for all the grief I've caused you both. And your ma, too. But Jesus has made a new man out of me, and He can do that for you, too. I haven't 'gone off the deep end' like the family says I have. But I brought you here tonight to tell you that I love you enough to want to share Jesus with you no matter what it costs me.

Wouldn't you like to at least think about it and maybe do the same?"

Roy was young and impressionable and could be swayed. He was about to open his mouth and reply positively when Don saw it coming and gave him a kick under the table.

"No, we wouldn't!" Don replied for them both.

"Guess not," Roy seconded weakly.

"I'm going to tell you something then," Joe responded. "A whole lot of people are going to be praying for both of you. Things happen when God's people get together and pray for somebody. When things happen to you, I want you to remember that a lot of people care about you and care that you find Jesus. Someday, because of those prayers, God is going to catch up with you both."

"If that God is Jesus," Don replied, "there's not a chance."

"We'll see, Son. Let's go. I'll take you home."

Sometime later Joe was notified that Sarah had begun divorce proceedings and planned to keep custody of the boys. His new faith had apparently cost him everything.

Chapter Sixteen
What Will It Take?

Roy moved quickly and stealthily down the dark halls of
Temple Israel. He had broken in through a window and now
headed for the liquor closet. He remembered that the synagogue stored several cases of liquor there for holiday times.
Roy, at fifteen, and his older brother, Don, were interested in
two things: alcohol and girls.

Roy, with his red hair and blue eyes, took on many of his
father's features. And he was less serious than Don, who at age
nineteen was moody, directionless in life, and given to bouts
with despondency.

It seemed strange to be back at Temple Israel, even if his
present purpose for being there hadn't been so bizarre. Roy
had not returned there since his Bar Mitzvah two years earlier. Like Don, he felt his obligation to Judaism ended on that
day. He was able to please his grandparents and do what nice
Jewish boys do; but for Roy, formal Judaism had ceased.

His Bar Mitzvah had been almost a comedy. Actually, it
was merely the closing act of a play. Beginning three years
earlier when he started Hebrew School, that whole experience
had left him with a larger-than-life hole inside of him. To his
Hebrew School teacher, Mr. Feinberg, Judaism was nothing
more than Zionism, Israel bonds and the Jewish national
anthem. The two-hour session that met several times a week
was occupied mainly with the monotonous study of the Hebrew language. Spiritual hunger was evidenced in few students; if it had been there at one time, it had vanished from
neglect. Since Mr. Feinberg had few answers to a spiritual
quest, a student's curiosity was dampened and any longing for
spiritual awareness was generally squelched before it had time
to raise its head.

Mr. Feinberg must have broken two dozen pencils over Roy Lessin. Calling on Roy to read part of the lesson for the day, Mr. Feinberg anxiously waited for some response from him; but he could seldom fulfill that assignment. Seldom listening in class, he rarely did any of the take-home assignments. Instead, he stared out the window, resenting the fact that he couldn't play baseball with his friends.

Mr. Feinberg would wait impatiently for Roy to answer his question. He paced the room and fussed with his hearing aid. Finally he came and stood at Roy's desk and tapped the pencil on it nervously. Why was this kid so stubborn and rebellious?

Everyone chuckled behind their books because they had watched this scene repeated so many times. Why should the teacher think that today was any different than yesterday? Roy, like Don, struggled with his Jewishness and the trouble it caused him; he resented even more this waste of time in Hebrew School over things that didn't matter to him.

He squirmed in his chair, though he felt some delight in his ability to irritate his teacher. Then came the standard reply: "I cannot read the assignment because I haven't done it yet."

Everyone, including Mr. Feinberg, already knew that this was always the pattern. And to everyone but the teacher, this scene was the one hope of comic relief for an incredibly boring two hours.

"Ach, Lessin!" came the predicted reply from Mr. Feinberg. Then he took the pencil he'd been tapping on Roy's desk and broke it in two.

"Get out of here!" he commanded. No longer even attempting to stifle it, everyone howled with laughter. Throwing Roy Lessin out of class was just as routine as opening the class with the "Hatikva," the Jewish national anthem!

Roy always managed to round up someone else in the building for a poker game until the bus left for home—usually another student had been thrown out with equal hopeless frustration, and together they found a dark room in Temple Israel for a card game. They savored the fact that they had the ability to make their teachers so hopelessly angry and thwarted.

But eventually Roy's passivity caught up with him. Three

years later at his Bar Mitzvah, he was going to be called upon to make a speech and read from the Hebrew prayer book! Not wishing to hurt his mother and other relatives and friends, he approached the Rabbi with his dilemma. A quick solution was found: Rabbi Aaronson would record the portion of the service in which Roy was involved. Roy would listen to it repeatedly until he had it completely memorized.

The big day arrived. At thirteen, he had reached the age of responsibility; dozens of family members and friends sat proudly out in the audience. He couldn't let them down. When he was called on, Roy opened the Hebrew prayer book, staring blankly at its Hebrew pages. Then he began to recite everything he had memorized from the recording.

Smiling faces beamed in the audience. Rabbi Aaronson came up behind Roy when he finished and put his arm around him. Finally he turned to the audience.

"Let us pray that this will be just the beginning for Roy Lessin, and that he will now go much deeper into his Judaism."

Heads nodded approval; Roy closed the prayer book and, just like Don had done four years earlier, silently made up his mind that he would have little or no involvement in synagogue activities for a long time!

But he was *not* finished with God. Had some strange curse, this questioning, been handed down from father to son? Just like Joe, Roy couldn't accept an eternity of nothingness, millenniums of blackness. There had to be a heaven and, if that was the case, there was an alternative to heaven. Having accepted the fact that God exists and that eternity rests in His hands, Roy knew there had to be a day of reckoning. There must be some way by which God judged individuals worthy of heaven or guilty of hell.

He decided that the Ten Commandments were the most likely basis of salvation. The law became his hope. God was just, he had been told by Rabbi Aaronson, so God would keep a balance sheet for Roy. As long as he kept more commandments than he broke, Roy figured he would "qualify" for heaven. And if he didn't fully understand one of the commandments, he put that one on the plus side, figuring that God wouldn't hold him accountable for something he didn't understand. Then he was careful to order his life in such a way that the positive outweighed the negative. Roy was careful, however, to leave room for a few commandments to be broken.

It was a convenient method of salvation for one who wanted a sizable foot in the world; he merely had to be cautious that the scales didn't tip too heavily the wrong way.

Now back to the halls of Temple Israel: Roy was experiencing a strange nostalgia for the things of God. He reflected on many issues as he worked on the lock of the liquor closet.

His peers were in a frantic search for meaning and purpose to life. They were unanimously convinced that the answer didn't lie with God, however. None of them could figure out why they were here or where they were going. They were of the "now" generation—interested only in the moment and all they could get from it. Their thoughts were totally secular.

Roy "tuned out" his reflective mood and concentrated on getting the cases of drinks back out the window without being caught. He knew what he was doing was definitely on the negative side of his "list," but he would be careful tomorrow in order to make up for it. Besides, all this liquor would make a party to end all parties!

Safely out of the Temple with his loot, Roy's thoughts turned to his dad. Joe had become much more than a simple irritation to Don and Roy. Only out of duty did they consent to see him, for he turned every visit into an opportunity to preach Jesus to them. After each such occasion the wall of resentment they felt for him grew higher. They chose to accept the family's conclusion about their dad: he believed things that no self-respecting Jew would consider. Don tuned Joe out altogether, and Roy discounted much of what his dad said except for things related to Israel. Joe told them what the Bible said about Israel and this intrigued Roy. Israel was going to be restored and the people brought back to the land; the desert would blossom again. Some fulfillment to those predictions could already be seen. A land to the north, Russia perhaps, was going to invade Israel someday and be destroyed. But some of the predictions lost some credibility with Roy when he was told that a turning to Jesus by the Jews was also a part of that plan outlined in the Bible.

Roy and Don chose another path of temporary fulfillment; their lives centered on parties, liquor, girls and "good times." Roy was not yet fourteen when he realized that he liked life a whole lot more when he was drunk. Besides, he followed the pace set by Don.

Don drank to escape reality. He was convinced he was nobody heading nowhere and that he had nothing to offer anybody. He felt inferior, worthless and directionless and was constantly reminded of that by his family. They called him a good-for-nothing disgrace and he believed them.

Retreating into a shell, he played with his fears and insecurities until they loomed larger than life. Just out of high school, his horizons admittedly were no greater than television and parties; Sarah supported him and the relatives washed their hands of him.

But somebody had to share Don's wretchedness. He chose those closest to him, Sarah and Roy. His verbal abuses flew at his mother more frequently now, sending her to her room in tears repeatedly. In his heart he knew that she was the best mother she could be. She worked full time to provide for their needs and make up for their dad's absence. But Don was killing his mother with his hatred and bitterness. He knew it and hated himself all the more.

Something inside wouldn't let him love or feel compassion. He saw himself accurately as a selfish, purposeless young man who hated life.

Because of this inward turmoil, at eighteen his hair began to fall out, and his skin was blemished with nerve-related problems. His self-image deteriorated even more as he saw himself in the mirror, old before he had even left his teens.

The pain of it all was lessened only when he drank heavily. Thoughts, feelings, frustrations were deadened as long as he poured down the alcohol.

And Roy was going to be just like his big brother, except that at fourteen, he could not handle large doses of liquor.

Drinking too much one afternoon, Roy literally tore the house apart. He turned into a wild man, beginning by knocking over every piece of furniture in his mother's apartment. Then he pulled out all the pots, pans and dishes from cupboards. After tearing up the bedding, he finally vomited throughout the house. Don managed to come home just in time to clean up the mess before their mother came home.

Don could do nothing but defend his younger brother, for his own behavior was just as obstinate. Somehow they had to stand by one another, united in their dislike for their dad and all he stood for.

Joe despaired over his sons; if ever there were two unlikely candidates for the kingdom of God, it was Roy and Don Lessin.

Don was also an unlikely choice for president of the Shantels. Twenty-five high school and college boys had organized in an elaborate way to throw the biggest, most impressive parties in town. Social events were complete with champagne machines, waiters, decorations and plenty of liquor for everyone. The Shantels were a family to one another as they rallied around their common interests: a respectable future, career and a desire to impress the sharpest girls in East Los Angeles. All had similar goals—all, that is, except their head, Don Lessin. He remained directionless and yet they looked to him for leadership. Perhaps it was because he was a good listener and everyone could dump his problems and concerns on him. He certainly had no answers, but he had a sympathetic ear.

The Shantels were careful about whom they allowed into the club. They wanted no losers, no one who would damage their image with the girls. They were all respectable guys when they were sober; when they were drunk, however, they became lewd and violent even in public.

Roy thumbed through his elaborate card file on all the girls he'd taken out. The Shantels were planning a New Year's Eve party and Roy had seen to it that they would all have plenty to drink. He wanted to match the perfect girl with the occasion. His card file of sixty names told him who he'd taken out, where they had gone, how much money he had spent, what the girl was like, and what she liked to do. For this party, she *must* like to drink. After all, he'd just risked his neck at Temple Israel!

Don sat staring at the television a few feet away, looking at but not seeing anything on the screen. As usual, he was lost in his private world. He seemed to be nursing some secret wounds and wanted no interruptions. Roy was preoccupied with his card file; Joe obviously had picked a poor time to drop in on them.

Roy rolled his eyes as Joe came in the door and Don turned up the television, hoping to drown out his dad's predicted religious chatter. Joe went straight to the television and angrily turned it off.

He always faced a dilemma: should he lower the boom on his sons for their behavior, or should he be gentle and patient in hopes that he might win them to the Lord more quickly? At the moment, the latter seemed impractical, for Joe knew that they were both slowly killing their mother with their attitude and life-style.

"You can believe everything the family says about me," Joe said without introduction and with rising anger, "but you *cannot* treat your mother the way you are doing! She tells me she spends most of her time crying about you guys. You can hate me and the rest of the world, but you can't take it out on her. Do you understand?"

There was awkward silence.

"Don't keep bugging us," Don finally muttered as he opened another beer.

"Let us work things out for ourselves," Roy said with less rancor.

"I may be a renegade to the family," Joe continued, "but you guys sure are no angels." He looked sternly at Don. "You've been out of school for months and all you do is slouch around and hurt your mother. You—"

"I'm getting out of everyone's hair pretty soon!" Don interrupted nastily. "I'm leaving for the Army Reserves in a few weeks. I'll be gone for six months."

Joe softened his approach. How could he expect his boys to

change their behavior without Jesus? "I'll say it again," he said more gently. "You don't have to like me, but you have to love your mother. She breaks her back for you two."

Don and Roy knew it was so. But Don in particular had nothing within himself that responded to love. He had little control over his attitudes and actions. He had never been able to bring himself to say "I love you." He wouldn't ask anyone's forgiveness. He could sit in the living room for hours and listen to his mother's weeping in her room. He seemed nailed to his chair. Part of him wanted to make it right with his mother, but he seemed unable to react, and the ensuing guilt feelings were turned on himself. Eaten away with anger, bitterness, resentment and self-pity, Don was Roy's only example and pattern in life.

But Roy's heart was not yet hardened, though he admittedly was on a downward spiral. He hoped that meaning and purpose to life would come by way of love and marriage. If he could just someday find the right girl and marry her, his searching would probably be over. That is why he was meticulously studying his card file of girls, for he pinned all his hopes for the future on one of them.

Joe turned to leave but looked once more at Don.

"I want you to be as good to your mother as you are to your drinking buddies."

Don looked away, inwardly cringing as he realized his dad had hit the nail on the head. Joe shook his head and again left in despair, wondering what it would take to bring his boys to Jesus.

Chapter Seventeen

A Seed Is Planted

"A lot of people will be praying for you, Son," Joe told Don the night before he left for Ft. Ord. Don, annoyed, refused to respond to such silly sentimentality! Then his dad, adding insult to injury, encouraged Don himself to pray as difficulties arose during his six-month stint in the Army Reserves.

"Pray and then watch things happen," Joe said that night, with his usual missionary zeal.

Weeks later that aggravating conversation came back to Don as he stared at the bunk above him. A raging toothache had prevented him from sleeping the last two nights. He'd had enough of the usual scrapes in life to be acquainted with pain, but this was agony unlike any of the others. Starting out as a dull ache, it had turned into a pounding, piercing pain that made his whole head throb and his stomach nauseated. Pain pills hadn't touched it. Nothing eased the discomfort and he wallowed in misery.

Maybe his dad's God could help. Don admitted to himself that he must be desperate to entertain *that* idea. Should he swallow his pride and offer a desperation prayer to some nebulous God? It couldn't do any permanent damage. What did he have to lose? Besides, nobody would ever have to know.

He made a feeble, awkward attempt. "God, if you're all you're cracked up to be, take away this toothache."

There, that was short and sweet and to the point. Don was sure nothing would change.

But the toothache was *instantly* gone! Not only was the discomfort gone, but Don felt totally exhilarated—on top of the world physically and mentally! And he felt as though he had had some kind of a spiritual experience. Surely it was coincidence! Just extraordinary timing, or his mind playing psychological tricks on him. Then again, could it have been Don's first encounter with God?

But by the time the bell jarred him from his sleep at 6:00 a.m. the next morning, he had rejected the whole experience.

Sinking more deeply into his inner conflicts, he now rebelled at every rule and regulation out of defiance and a hatred for himself and the Army. He turned up in formation with his uniform on backwards and his shoes deliberately scuffed. He fought every order and spent the next six months washing pots and pans because of his rebellion. Six months of submission was nearly the living end for Don. It was a fate far worse, Don was sure, than his dad's description of hell. He would be a six-year private in the Reserves, having no desire to rise in rank or status. He wanted the whole experience over quickly without having to experience the alternative: two years of active duty overseas.

Back in Los Angeles Roy wallowed in similar uncertainty; now he didn't have his brother, either, for company or sympathy. But he *did* have his handy dating card file and his hope that love and marriage would be the answer.

He walked hand in hand with Rochelle one evening on a Los Angeles sidewalk. His friend Marty with Marlene, his date, walked a few steps behind them. Latecomers still streamed into a nearby stadium, though the foursome's destination was anything but this Billy Graham Crusade. But a voice could be heard over the loudspeaker, coming from inside. Something drew Roy's attention to the words and he slowed his pace.

"What do you think is going on in there?" Roy called back to his friends curiously.

"Some Bible-thumping fanatic is preaching, I think," Marty replied. "Come on, let's keep moving."

Marty and his date walked ahead several yards as Roy hung behind for a few moments. Rochelle was obviously irritated.

That voice over the loudspeaker was preaching about Jesus again. He spoke about the wretchedness and the hopelessness of humanity apart from a Savior. The voice said that Jesus was the only hope for the world, but that most of the world shut Him out of their lives.

It was a familiar theme to Roy Lessin—one that he had automatically tuned out a hundred times when Joe preached it. What made him want to hang behind and listen?

"Lessin, come on!" Marty yelled impatiently. "Don't tell me you're interested in that Jesus stuff!"

He listened pensively another few seconds until Rochelle jerked his hand.

"Not a chance, buddy!" Roy replied cockily. Then he turned to Rochelle. "Let's get out of here."

They moved on, but Roy's heart secretly lingered wistfully back at that stadium. It was unexplainable to him.

"Did you really think you could find any answers back there?" Rochelle asked curiously. She was a nice Jewish girl who wanted nothing to do with God, much less Jesus.

"No, I don't think so," Roy said defensively.

"Well, if you ever do find some answers," she said, "let me know. Wherever it lies, I'll become a disciple of it. I just hope the answer doesn't lie in religion of any kind. That is deadly dull!"

Roy struggled to gather his thoughts and energies back toward having a good time, but his heart wasn't in it that night.

Chapter Eighteen

A Plan for My Life?

Don intended to take advantage of his first weekend free since joining the Army. He had been denied almost every free time because of his behavior. But this weekend he came back to L.A. to look up some of his old drinking buddies. Somehow he would make up for lost time and live recklessly for two full days.

Don and his buddies chatted excitedly as they tore down Highway 101 in his mother's car. They had a lot of catching up to do. All liked to live dangerously and drink heavily. Already they had had too many drinks. David had drunk the least and felt that maybe he should drive, but Don seemed to be managing all right. Next to David sat Mike, an Army friend of Don's.

It was the first time in months Don felt like life had been handed back to him. The combination of his exuberance and the alcohol made his foot rather heavy on the gas pedal. A steady rain fell, making Highway 101 unusually slick in the gathering darkness.

Don tore confidently down a hill.

"Hey, buddy, take it easy," Mike said, an edge of fear in his voice.

"I can handle it," Don replied.

"So what's the hurry?" Mike asked. "We've got all weekend."

Mike and Dave glanced at one another cautiously. Enthusiasm had quickly turned to carelessness.

Suddenly they rounded a curve and stared head-on into the headlights of an on-coming car that was taking as many chances as Don. Both swerved in a last-minute effort to avoid a collision, but it was too late. Don threw his arms in front of his face.

The sickening screech of tires, screams, metal hitting metal, and breaking glass was finally overtaken by an eerie silence. It had been a bull's-eye head-on crash.

Mike had been sent through the windshield with deadly speed. Dave had flown out a door and Don out the window of his door.

Lying motionless on the highway as the rain drenched him, Don stared into the blackness above him and listened to the moans and cries of the wounded and the sounds of traffic on the highway. He wondered why he was alive. Why didn't his body scream with pain? Had he perhaps been paralyzed? Maybe he was bleeding to death there on the highway with an arm or a leg severed and his neck broken! He wanted to call out to his friends, but he was afraid that their silence would mean they were dead.

Finally a siren could be heard in the distance. He heard a feeble call for help—maybe someone in the other car.

The shriek of the siren grew louder.

Don was sure the Highway Patrol would run right over him as he lay sprawled out on the road in the rain. At last a police car stopped near Don, its lights flashing, and he heard footsteps racing toward him. A flashlight beamed in his face.

"Can you move, kid?" the uniformed man asked.

"I don't know," Don replied.

"Do you feel any pain?"

"No. Could I be paralyzed?"

The two officers carefully lifted Don to his feet. The flashlight beam moved all around him looking for wounds. Don realized that all his senses seemed to be normal.

"Lady luck was with you this time," one officer said. "All I see is a minor cut on your head."

They abandoned Don for the other victims, who were much more seriously injured. Sirens wailed for an hour as the injured were rushed away, some with massive wounds.

The impact between the two vehicles had been most severe on Don's side, and yet he was hardly scratched. Why? He watched as the others were placed in ambulances and whisked away down the highway, racing against the clock. His buddy,

Mike, was critically injured from having gone through the windshield. So why should Don Lessin get a break in life?

Finally a highway patrol car took him back to his mother's apartment. Both Sarah and Joe had been notified and they paced nervously back and forth until Don arrived. Gathering himself together, he tried to cover up the whole frightening ordeal with his usual arrogance, wiping away every visible appearance of fear.

"Pretty lucky, huh?" He swaggered in confidently, sporting just two Band-Aids.

"It's not luck!" Joe protested. "It's God. He doesn't want you dead for some reason. Maybe He has some crazy plan for your life."

Predictably, Don was annoyed. "So now you're telling me that it was the hand of God that spared me, right?" He continued sarcastically, "One of His angels hovered over me. Is that it?"

"That's right," Joe answered quietly.

The highway patrolman interrupted the awkward scene.

"I've seen hundreds of accidents like yours, kid," he said as he moved towards the door to leave. "The fact that you're alive is one of the more incredible miracles I've ever seen. I don't care how you all interpret what happened. But I'm telling you how I see it, and I speak from experience. Everybody should be dead, and you should have gone first."

Don shrugged his shoulders and went to his room, inwardly concerned over the fate of his buddies. But nobody would see any kind of emotion written on him. He remained his stoic, embittered self in spite of the accident and the so-called "miracle" aspect of it.

Yet he couldn't brush it off. He couldn't bury the whole scene away in some remote corner of his mind. It wouldn't leave him alone. In moments of complete candidness, the whole thing bothered and haunted him. So did his dad's strange comment: "Maybe God has some crazy plan for your life."

Could it be? Still imprisoned by the Army, he couldn't get drunk, either, to drown out such annoying thoughts.

Chapter Nineteen

A Better Jew

Months of rebellion and bitterness turned into years for Roy and Don Lessin. Roy followed his brother's footsteps as he had always done. The draft was ahead for him and, upon Don's suggestion, he also decided to get the whole thing over with in the six-month Reserve program.

Joe saw less and less of his sons, though the prayer vigil for them had increased. At moments he was less discouraged over them, and at those times he was sure they couldn't escape the hand of God in their lives as believers prayed over them both daily.

But there was little outward evidence that either of them had mellowed to the gospel. Their riotous, irresponsible life-style intensified by the week. They both embraced a cynicism which left no room for serious thought. Living only for the moment, they desperately looked for "a good time." Don seemed to be hopelessly locked into defiant rebellion toward all authority and responsibility, though Roy still had a corner of his heart that hadn't totally rejected his dad.

Roy paced back and forth outside the Statler Hilton in Los Angeles? Why had he consented to come, anyway? Joe had been strangely persuasive when he invited Roy to attend a meeting of the International Convention of the Gideons. His dad was to be one of the speakers, though Roy had no idea what that was all about. But he was impressed with Joe's sincerity in wanting to see him once more before Roy left for Ft. Ord.

So what did he have to lose? Roy would slip in a back row, hear his dad out, then shake hands with him and be out of sight and hearing for six months.

The crowd swallowed him up as he made his way into the

huge auditorium. He felt awkward and out of place with these Christians who seemed to tote their Bibles around like weapons and who appeared much too clean and polished to know the first thing about life. He felt terribly uncomfortable around these naive Gentiles. In spite of his previous rationale, he decided this had been a mistake after all. He should have listened more carefully to his family's warnings: his dad was into something that Jews should avoid at all costs.

Joe was already seated on the platform and spotted Roy in the auditorium. He visibly beamed at Roy upon eye contact, pleased that his son had made it. Roy's heart sank, then pounded more furiously. Why couldn't he have Don's brashness and just tear out of here, anyway? The crowd pushed him along toward a seat much farther toward the front than he intended. On the way strangers stopped and introduced themselves to him, which seemed unusual. What was it they wanted? They seemed genuinely warm and friendly, and Roy concluded that they only wanted his soul to display somewhere like an athletic trophy. Their smiles and handshakes were genuine, it appeared, but Roy was convinced that more sinister motives lay beneath the surface.

An hour of preliminaries in the program nearly put him to sleep. What a way to spend his last day of freedom! Somehow he had let himself get trapped in the center of a row; it was impossible to get out without attracting too much attention.

Finally his dad stepped behind the podium. Anger and disinterest caused Roy to blank out nearly everything Joe was saying. Just a few opening phrases reminded Roy that the family's evaluation of Joe Lessin was accurate: he'd become a Gentile and he expounded things that Jews would never accept.

Roy fidgeted and watched the clock. Hadn't he put in enough time yet?

"I have a son who is going into the Army tomorrow." Joe's words from the podium suddenly caught Roy's attention. "He doesn't know the Lord. I love this son very much. His name is Roy, and I'd like you all to pray for him in the coming weeks. I want him to know the peace of our Lord Jesus as I have come to know it."

Roy couldn't believe his ears! How could his dad pull such a stunt on him? He wanted to dig a trapdoor and disappear through the floor. He was sure that all eyes were on him now, like a pack of vultures about to descend and eat him alive.

The program ended abruptly and Joe made his way toward his son. Roy finally was realizing that Joe had done it out of love and hadn't meant to embarrass him. But why couldn't Christians just keep to themselves and give up their missionary zeal toward those they were certain were "lost"? The Jews didn't go about proselytizing. They were content to let everybody stay just where they were, hoping the world would take their religious cue from them.

"I wish you hadn't done that," Roy muttered to his dad as they met in the aisle.

"I want you to take this Bible with you," Joe said, disregarding Roy's comment.

"It's no use, Dad. You know I won't read it. Why don't you give up?"

"Take it anyway," Joe said warmly. "You never know when you might want to draw from it. It has a lot of wisdom in it whether you agree with the Bible or not!"

Roy reluctantly took the book from Joe.

"Son, I want you to know that a lot of people are praying for you every day, especially now as you leave. I told your brother that once, too. Things have happened to him, but he always chooses to disregard the fact that God was involved in them. Don't be as stiff-necked as Don is. You might save yourself some grief, Roy. Let God reveal himself to you while there is still time."

His dad was coming on as usual like the prophet of doom he always was. The world would end someday soon, Jesus was going to come back, and Roy and Don would be left behind! It sounded like good science fiction! If Joe's Bible told stories like that, why should Roy Lessin give the Bible an ounce of credibility by accepting it from his dad?

And yet an almost magnetic force kept the Bible in Roy's hand.

"Okay," he said to Joe as they shook hands in parting. "I've got to run. I'll probably have a few weekends off, and I'll come back to L.A. I'll give you a call."

Roy knew that it was unlikely he would complete that promise; but the words would make his dad feel good. Roy realized how much Joe had suffered from the misunderstanding and rejection of his family. It impressed Roy that his dad went right on loving each member of the family, even though they ridiculed him.

He tossed restlessly in the same barracks where Don had a few years earlier.

"Lessin, relax!" Nate whispered loudly in the bunk next to him.

"I can't."

"What's wrong?"

Roy thought for several moments and realized he didn't know what was wrong. He knew he was disgusted with Army life. Every week Roy managed to violate some regulation that kept him from going home on leave. Many of his violations weren't deliberate as Don's had been. But circumstances seemed to be against him, and he felt like some diabolical committee had been formed to make Army life miserable for him. No matter what he did, it backfired on him and he was stuck scrubbing floors on his day off.

Nathan was his only comfort. Also Jewish, Nate had just enough of a spiritual vacuum within him that he willingly participated in occasional spiritual dialogue with Roy. Finally Roy sat up on his bunk and faced his buddy. Now it had dawned on him what was bothering him.

"Humanity is rotten to the core," Roy said quietly so he didn't awaken the men around him. Roy had concluded that the Army was an accurate cross-section of humanity, and these soldiers revealed life to be a cesspool of immorality, evil and selfishness. In the six weeks that he'd been at Ft. Ord, he had seen nothing but cheating, lying, stealing, fighting, perversion, cursing and lewdness. Immorality permeated almost every conversation and seemed to lie behind each motive.

Roy clearly saw that if all the stops were pulled out, man would choose to live like an animal with only selfish goals.

With little sense of right or wrong, men were basically evil.

But not Roy! He still had his handy method of righteousness as long as he *kept* more of the Ten Commandments than he *broke*! He could still add up at least *six* commandments that he kept and only four that he broke, so he was still on the winning edge!

"So why has it taken you all this time to figure out that men are so rotten?" Nate asked. "You've been around enough, Lessin, to know that life has a lot of corruption. And you've been a willing participant in a lot of it!"

Roy didn't answer for several moments.

"What do you say we go to Shabbat services tomorrow night," he finally suggested to Nate. "Besides, I want to get out of duty here at the barracks and that's the only sure way I know of. What do you say?"

"Only you would get religious in the Army!" Nate scoffed. "But if it makes you feel better, we'll go."

What was this tiny seed of spiritual hunger doing within Roy anyway? He reached into the drawer by his bunk and pulled out that Bible. Then he dug around until he found a flashlight and turned it on the Bible.

"What do you see in that book, Lessin?" Nate asked curiously.

"I've never looked at it before," Roy admitted. "I'm not sure why I even brought it along. I've ridiculed everything my dad believes in, yet I accepted a Bible. Strange, isn't it?"

"You need a weekend off, that's all. The Army is getting to you because all you do on your days off is scrub floors and kettles."

"What do you think about Israel?" Roy asked, ignoring Nate's assessment.

"Haven't thought much about it. Maybe it would be a nice place to visit some day."

"My dad says that Israel becoming a nation is the fulfillment of Bible prophecy."

He slowly glanced through the Bible as the flashlight batteries began to dim. He shook it, hoping that it would hold out a few more moments so he could read.

"I'll admit I'm interested in prophecy like that," Roy con-
fessed to Nate who was too sleepy to carry on the conversation.
"My dad says the book of Revelation is all about prophecy.
Have you ever looked at Revelation?"

Nate aimlessly nodded his head and drifted off to sleep.
Roy flipped to the back of the Bible and began to read some
verses out of Revelation. Most of it made no sense, but what
he *did* understand frightened him enough to keep reading! According to this mysterious book, *great* judgments were to come
upon the earth and upon mankind! Didn't the world deserve
those judgments? An hour earlier, Roy had told Nate how
wicked and perverse he saw humanity. Now the book of Revelation agreed with that and, furthermore, promised severe
punishment on corrupt mankind.

He slammed the Bible shut and leaned back on his pillow.
Sleep was hopeless now. His mind raced in high gear and his
heart pounded. What assurance did Roy Lessin have that *he*
wouldn't be a part of this kind of judgment? What if his scale
of measurement, his Ten-Commandment method of salvation, tipped too far the wrong way? What if he had counted in-
correctly? What if he was a victim of the judgments pro-
nounced on humanity in the book of Revelation?

Perhaps the answer was in Judaism, just as Rabbi Aaronson had said years earlier. Roy could hardly wait for the Shabbat service that next evening. That *had* to be the answer, at
least in part. Roy could live with the idea of being a better
Jew—never, however, with being a goy like his dad. But it
would please his family if Roy embraced more of his Judaism.

Finally with that decided he was able to close his eyes and
drift into a light sleep. He would be a better Jew and that
gnawing fear and uncertainty within him would surely ease.

Chapter Twenty

Your Sons Will Come From Afar

The fact that some silly group of people calling themselves the "Burden-Bearers" were praying daily for Roy made him nearly double up in laughter. But then, what could it hurt? Maybe their petitions would actually amount to something and gain him some answers. His sincere but brief exploration into Judaism had been unsatisfying. He had obtained no answers to life from Judaism's ritual and tradition. No peace of mind had come, and no purpose or direction in life had been received.

Nothing changed, in fact, except that Roy, like Don, had grown more frustrated, cynical and angry because of the Army. Years stretched ahead of them with two nights a week and a Sunday a month having to be given up for something that only embittered them. They were both so opposed to the disciplines forced upon them by this system that they further drowned themselves in liquor to make it bearable. Then they showed up at Reserve meetings drunk and were routinely chewed out by their officers. Don and Roy deliberately and definitely would remain eight-year privates.

Too confined by living with their mother, they now moved into an apartment together across the street from Valley College in the San Fernando Valley. Roy held on for dear life to the only option left for fulfillment in life: love and marriage. But in order for him to experience that, he had to give serious consideration to a career. It would require little effort to attend classes across from his apartment, so he enrolled at Valley College with a physical education major. If it would help him find the right girl to marry, he would aim towards becoming a football coach.

Within weeks of their new apartment living, Roy's bubble

152

burst. Every married couple in the building was unfaithful to each other. Roy's "ideal couple" in the building was involved in out-and-out prostitution. Couples changed partners faster than Roy could keep track. Eventually he didn't know which couple belonged together and figured the whole building was involved in some kind of musical partners or group immorality. What had happened to love and marriage? It was one thing to carry on like this while single; it was something else when married.

Don had one ear to the television, but seemed much more interested in the six-pack of beer he was finishing. At twenty-two he was still floundering, without direction and motivated by nothing.

"The Mitchells were at it again last night," Roy remarked. "They fight an awful lot."

Don didn't respond.

"What guarantee do I have," Roy asked more loudly, "that my wife and I won't do the same thing?"

"So who's getting married?" Don shrugged, an eye still on the television.

"I am some day," Roy replied weakly. "I'll find the right girl and settle down like everybody else does. Except I don't want my marriage to end up like those in this building."

"Life away from home got you a little apprehensive?" Don ridiculed. "Can't you take reality? Come on, you were in the Army for six months. You know nobody is an angel, single or married!"

Don's own fears and insecurities kept him from even considering marriage. His life-style was too irresponsible and disjointed to complicate it with a serious relationship.

But Roy was sure that at one time, every quarreling couple in their apartment building had had his dream: a good marriage which would be the answer to everything.

So where were they all going wrong? Didn't *anybody* have harmony and peace in their lives? Everyone's problems seemed to be doubled now that they were married.

He left Don staring glassy-eyed at the television and walked to a nearby hot-dog stand, the cheapest food available.

After the rent was paid, all remaining cash went into their "alcohol fund." Hardly any money ever was left for groceries. Roy still had a foul taste in his mouth from having eaten a whole onion three days earlier—that was all the food they had in the house and neither of them had any money. A week earlier, Roy had gotten a slight case of food poisoning at this same hot-dog stand. As he had lain in his bed, wretchedly ill from the food poisoning and wallowing in self-pity, his own emptiness had enveloped him again like a suffocating blanket. Nobody had known he was sick except Don, and he hadn't seemed to care. No one had been around to dish out any sympathy to him like Sarah had always done—in spite of the way they had treated her.

He now headed back to the same food stand.

Roy knew he wanted to make it big in life. He wanted a home in Beverly Hills, with a swimming pool and three-car garage. He wanted the fanciest kind of car. The problem was that he didn't really want to work very hard for it. He figured he would hang onto the present and maybe win some magical sweepstakes or get a windfall from a rich relative.

One thing was clear, however: living on your own at nineteen wasn't very glamorous after all. Roy had been sure there was something very appealing about independence that early in life. It would be impressive, he had thought, to show off the bar he and Don had put in their apartment and to display their empty liquor bottles in every window and ledge. And it was impressive to hang pictures of nude women in every room.

But all this freedom hadn't brought satisfaction. And furthermore, in order to keep up the front and the fun and games, they both would have to resort to part-time work. Such distasteful reality could easily burst their rapidly deflating bubble!

Back at the apartment, Don tried to concentrate on the television program. Maybe he'd had too many beers. Was it laziness, or had something mellowed in him enough so that he didn't change the channel in spite of the religious nonsense being expounded on the Billy Graham Philadelphia Crusade? He usually despised such sentimentality and Bible preaching;

this time he felt almost captivated by it.

He even moved to turn up the volume. Not clear-headed enough to grasp much that was being said, his own inebriation and inability to concentrate muddled the words.

"Jesus said I am the way, the truth and the life." The preacher's words finally came into focus enough for Don to grasp, except that he would never accept that. So why did those words run through his head now like a tape-recorded message? Maybe another beer would drown them out.

Don couldn't turn away from the television screen. He threw an empty beer can at the wall in frustration, then leaned closer to the television. Everything the speaker said sounded familiar; in the past he would have walked away from such nonsense as he did whenever his dad preached it.

Now his whole, stoic and very fragile self-image was being shattered. A choir began to sing some emotional song in response to the preacher's "invitation." Thousands of people streamed forward inside the giant stadium, to be "born again."

Tears streamed down Don's face. Some folks didn't leave their seats and Don realized he wanted *everybody* to go forward! Even if *he* could never agree to such Christian nonsense, he wanted everybody in that stadium to do what the speaker asked them to do. They were all Gentiles, Don was sure, and all the Gentiles should be "born again." It sounded good to him—sort of a fresh start in life. It made sense for the first time that the Gentiles should let Jesus transform their lives.

He angrily switched off the television before he totally succumbed to his own emotion. There was a knock on the door and he quickly wiped away the tears that made his whole face shine.

What rotten timing. It was Joe who came in right on the heels of Billy Graham! This was too much.

Joe was visibly shaken by the overwhelming presence of a pleasure-seeking world in his two sons' apartment. Now that they were on their own, it appeared they had pulled out all the plugs. He could see by the liquor bottles, beer cans and pornographic pictures and calendars that his sons were steeped much deeper in sin than he had realized. He choked back the tears as he greeted Don.

"You really like living like this?" he asked brokenly.

"Why not?" Don snapped, irritated by his dad's visit.

Joe searched for the right words. He hadn't seen Don in weeks and didn't want to fall into an immediate argument.

"Don't you think you're old enough now, Son, to be a responsible adult?" he asked gently.

"So who says I'm not?" his son replied coldly. "Roy and I are supporting ourselves. We're not taking handouts. We pay the rent on time. What more should we be doing? If you want us to be a part of the great American way of life, you may be disappointed. We want to enjoy life." The words rang hollow even to Don.

"Live for today and get all you can, no matter who gets hurt, right?"

"Well, something like that. But we're not hurting anybody."

Don walked to the empty refrigerator then slammed it shut. He knew it had been empty an hour earlier, so what did he think had changed?

"*Jesus said I am the way.*" Who said that? Was it an inner voice?

"Don't bug us, Dad," he said defensively again. "Roy and I won't disgrace you. We won't take charity. Just quit trying to save our souls, okay?"

Joe turned away from the often-repeated scene. Too many times he'd come to show his sons the love of God, but he had to leave defeated and heavy-hearted. This was no exception.

Joe despaired too much to even drive away. He sat in his car pouring out his heart to God. Every time he saw his boys it appeared they had gone deeper into sin and rebellion. Remembering his own stubbornness, he tried to take heart in the fact that many were praying for Don and Roy. And yet Joe Lessin was losing faith that his sons would ever come to Jesus.

His tears turned the world before him into blurry images as he sat in his car, barely able to make out the chapters in the Bible as he opened it randomly. God had to see his desperation and give him a shred of hope. That wasn't asking too much, was it? Outwardly, all hope was gone.

Wiping some tears away he looked down at Isaiah 60. He tried to focus his eyes on the words before him: "Lift up your eyes round about, and see: They all gather together, they come to you. Your sons will come from afar. . . . "

"Your sons will come from afar."

It *had* to be a direct word of comfort and encouragement from the Lord! His sons would come from afar (they seemed to be as far away as they could possibly get right now), and *they would come to Joe*. They would seek him out. It rekindled the flame of hope for Joe!

God had not forgotten Don or Roy Lessin!

Chapter Twenty-one

Does the Good Outweigh the Bad?

Roy watched the alarm clock tick slowly away. Even Don wasn't around to talk to, as he'd taken a part-time job from 2:00 to 5:00 a.m.

Roy had just met Sharon that week. He was very impressed with her: she was a nice girl who had "religion" and who attended a parochial college. He wanted to give her something before she went back to her school in a few days.

Sharon, however, wasn't on a religious bandwagon like his dad. But she was a good girl who had ideals, goals and a purpose in life. For some reason, Roy wanted to impress her more than the dozens of others who had come and gone in his life.

A Bible! Yes, a Bible would be a good thing to get her and it would make him look like her kind of guy. The Bible his Dad had given him when he went into the Army had somehow gotten lost, perhaps conveniently so. He wouldn't know how to begin to find a new one except that he knew his dad always had plenty of them on hand! Could Roy swallow his pride and ask Joe for one? It would probably work out all right as long as his dad clearly understood that the Bible was for Sharon and not Roy.

He paced his apartment while the world slept. Something else nagged at him but he couldn't define it. He mixed a drink, thinking it would either drown his thoughts or bring them more clearly to the surface.

He went back and sat on the edge of his bed, staring into the blackness. His jumbled thoughts finally crystalized: he had broken more of the Ten Commandments than he had kept! His whole basis for righteousness had just been shattered. The awful late-night revelation churning in his subconscious was this: Roy Lessin is just as rotten a sinner as everyone else!

He paced the floor again, as echoes of another marital quarrel resounded down the hall. He knew he had to face up to some unseen jury, and the verdict would be that he was more corrupt than he ever wanted to believe. Somehow Roy knew that if he were to stand before God that night and be judged on the basis of the law, he would be found guilty. And that made him a candidate for God's wrath and a sentence in hell. Roy had always insisted upon going his own way, and that clearly led him down a path of guilt and condemnation.

Setting the drink aside, he buried his head in his hands. He had never experienced anything like this before. He knew, somehow, that God was doing the convicting. Roy had been caught, tried and convicted. Sentencing awaited. There was only one place for selfish sinners like him.

There had to be a way out of the dilemma. What was it?

"God, show me what to do," he whispered softly. "Show me a way out." It was a simple, uncomplicated prayer, but it was sincere.

Stranger still, Roy actually *initiated* a meeting with his dad the next day. Roy generally avoided Joe and made up a hundred excuses so he wouldn't have to see him when Joe wanted to visit. And just as incredible, Roy was looking forward to the encounter. He anticipated pleasing both his dad and Sharon over the gift. It wasn't often in life that Roy accomplished anything but disappointing people.

He smelled the aroma of his dad's home-cooked meal as he pushed the door bell. There were other voices inside and that meant that he wouldn't be alone with his dad. Maybe it was just as well in case the conversation got too religious. He hadn't forgotten about the experience of the night before; it's just that Roy still wasn't ready to pursue Jesus or Christianity. He figured he would just spend a casual time with Joe, take the Bible for Sharon and then leave. In the daylight his sins didn't seem so bad after all. Maybe the experience in the blackness of the night was only an emotional overaction.

It was too late now. He was inside the door and surrounded by two or three strangers who seemed to know his whole life story. He imagined they were more of his dad's overbearing Christian friends who were after Roy's soul. The situation was painfully awkward; he mentally kicked himself for having initiated this whole scene. It was his own fault; why hadn't he listened more carefully to the warnings from his family?

"So you want another Bible?" Joe said immediately, wasting no time. He looked pleased, as did the strangers in the room. They all had looks on their faces that said they knew something Roy didn't know.

"It's not for me," Roy clarified quickly. "It's for this girl I met. She goes to a parochial school so I think she's religious."

"So it won't hurt you to take another look at the Bible either," Joe said, smiling at his son. "It contains all the answers to the questions you're asking."

"Who says I'm asking questions?" Roy asked defensively.

"I know you are," Joe replied quietly.

Roy plopped himself down in an overstuffed chair that nearly swallowed him up, and debated whether or not he should mention what had happened to him the night before. He didn't want to appear in any way eager to discuss religious things because he was sure Joe and his friends would pounce on him—another notch in their evangelistic guns. And yet, he admitted to himself, he *had* asked for God's help.

"Something happened to me last night," Roy finally confessed. Now there was no turning back.

"About 3:00 a.m. last night I realized I'd broken more of the Ten Commandments than I'd kept. You know, I always figured that if the good outweighed the bad, I'd be looked upon favorably by God in the end."

"Jesus doesn't want us to focus on our good works and deeds or on keeping the law," Joe answered. All eyes were on father and son. "Jesus accepts those of us who freely come to Him; in spite of all our sins, He can then transform us into new creatures. Sort of like the ugly worm that turns into a beautiful butterfly. That's why Jesus came to us. He came to atone for our sins and to forgive us for them just by our asking

Him. That way, *nobody* has to keep score of good vs. bad deeds. Anyway, Roy, even if our good deeds do outweigh the bad, we still are not acceptable to God. *All* our evil ways must be forgiven and forgotten. And the only way that can happen is through Jesus. He's the supreme sacrifice for the sins of the human race. It's that simple."

At any other time Roy would have abruptly closed a conversation like this. It was too risky; one follower of Jesus in the family was enough.

"But you have to *want* Him to make you that new creature," Joe continued. "You have to humble yourself, confess your sins, and ask Jesus to transform you."

Roy couldn't understand why he was listening with different ears today. Something inside of him said that he should listen to everything his dad said. What was more extraordinary, something inside of him whispered that his dad spoke the truth.

Roy tripped back into his familiar way of thinking and responded, "Frankly, I'm afraid of Don." He shifted nervously in his chair. "You know he will never go along with this. I simply can't alienate him."

Joe went on as though Roy had never protested or raised another argument. "There is no sin that is too grave for Jesus to forgive," he continued. "I think you are overwhelmed by your sins, Son. I think that God touched you last night and that He revealed your own wretchedness. You need to deal with all of that, because Jesus isn't going to let you go."

Roy softened.

"I'll admit I asked God to help me last night," he said slowly. "I guess I hoped God would help me someday, but I sure didn't figure that the answer would be with Jesus. I've thought all along that you and your friends are wrong. Well, maybe Christianity is okay for your Gentile friends—maybe even for you, though I've chosen to believe what the family says about that—especially Don. He has really strong feelings about your faith in Jesus. We can hardly discuss it. He just flies off the handle."

"But in your heart you know that everything I've said is true, don't you?" Joe asked pointedly.

There was a long pause as Roy counted the cost of his reply. He had to weigh carefully the expected results of a positive answer. He shifted again, looking at the ceiling and then at the floor. Finally his eyes looked right into his dad's.

"I think I do," he finally admitted. "Is it okay if I just *believe* it? Do you think things will be all right between God and me if I just *believe* what you're saying?"

"That's not enough, Son."

"Why not?"

Joe went to the kitchen and got a glass of water, then returned to the living room with his object lesson.

"If you were in a desert dying of thirst," he explained, "desperately needing a glass of water, and I walked up to you with this and held it before you, it would do you no good unless you drank it. Even though you *believe* it could save your life, you would still have to *drink* from it. That's the way it is with the Lord. You can't just believe things about Him; you've got to *receive* Him."

"I'll lose everything then," Roy said mournfully. "I'll lose Don and the rest of the family. I'll lose my friends. I'll lose just about everything. It's a high price. I don't know if I can pay it. Maybe," Roy, relieved, rose from his chair, "we can talk about it again another time."

"Roy, the Bible says that *today* is the day of salvation. You might not have another opportunity to respond to Jesus! Tomorrow isn't promised to anybody. Only today."

The truth of that prompted him to sit down again.

"Maybe we could just discuss this between ourselves," Roy said awkwardly, looking at the strangers in the room.

"God resists the proud, but shows himself to the humble, it says in the Bible," his dad answered. "You've been a proud young man. It would do you good to confess Jesus in front of these people here. They have all prayed for you many times."

Another minute of silence as Roy considered his options. Finally his dad broke in, "Son, you don't receive Jesus into your life like you take an aspirin tablet that solves some malady. Rather, you receive Him to become the Lord and Messiah of your life. He's not just another gimmick that we call on until we can go on to something better. He's not an experiment;

we can't return the package for a money-back guarantee if we're not satisfied. We give Him everything—the fears, insecurities, unanswered questions and our whole life. And in return, He promises to do a new thing in us. It's a sure thing, Roy. And I believe that your spiritual need is greater than all the excuses you're thinking about right now. In your own heart you know that it's all true, don't you?"

Roy reluctantly nodded in agreement.

"So would you like to pray to Jesus now?"

Roy took a deep breath. "I think I would, Dad."

Within moments, Roy Lessin knew that he had been in contact with the living God and that the relationship was right! Years of guilt were swept away. In the past, Roy would have scorned such simple faith, except that now he had experienced it; everything Joe had said over the years was exactly right. From head to foot, he felt the presence of God's love and forgiveness. He probably could never explain it completely to his friends. They would be just as skeptical as Roy had been over the years. Until one utterly risks and exercises that simple faith, understanding it all or intellectually analyzing it was virtually impossible. His peers were conditioned to think that *nothing* could be as simple as uttering a prayer and having a new kind of peace and hope permeate one's whole being.

But there was still apprehension within him as he left Joe's later that night. He thought about a verse his dad showed him in the Bible that said: "Whosoever therefore shall confess me before men, him will I confess also before my Father which is in heaven; but whosoever shall deny me before men, him will I also deny before my Father which is in heaven" (Matt. 10:32, 33).

Roy Lessin could *never* confess Jesus before his family. And yet Jesus required it!

The awful dread of that impending confrontation almost could cancel out his joy over the fact that his sins were now forgiven.

Chapter Twenty-two

I Am the Way

Roy decided that if he were confronted, he would not deny Christ, but he simply *couldn't* initiate the subject himself. Eventually, though, his changed behavior began to arouse curiosity and produce questions.

Overnight he quit drinking and cursing, the two things that had been a natural part of him for years. He recognized the incredible power of God in his life because of this change. And yet he was aware that he was not progressing in other areas of his walk with the Lord. In the two weeks he'd been a Christian, he hadn't read a Bible or gone to a church like his dad had urged him to do. Otherwise, Joe had left him pretty much alone those early weeks, sending a note now and then for encouragement but staying away from the apartment.

Don finally caught on to the obvious changes and began to act distant. He seemed preoccupied and distraught. He was silent for two full days and barely responded to Roy's attempts at conversation. He drank heavily, sinking deeper into his despondency. But it was Don himself who finally broke the ice and popped the inevitable question to Roy late one evening.

"When you were at Dad's a few weeks ago," he began, his eyes suspicious, "did you make some kind of spiritual commitment?"

Roy's heart nearly stopped beating. It had finally happened. Now he was faced with the very thing he dreaded the most: confirming or denying Jesus! Stalling for time, he tried to change the subject. It didn't work, however, with either Don *or* God.

His brother asked the pointed question again, this time with even more accusation in his voice. "Roy, have you made some kind of spiritual commitment?"

"Yes, I have."

There. It was over! He'd finally said it to another living soul! As feeble and subdued as his confession had been, Roy experienced a tremendous release, and the joy of his salvation almost overwhelmed him.

Don was thoroughly disgusted to have confirmed the fact of which he was already aware. "I thought so. When I did the laundry this week, a note Dad had sent you fell out of your jeans. In it he said something about your new walk with the Lord. I just had to hear it with my own ears, Roy. I think you're a colossal hypocrite!"

"How come?"

"For one thing, you smoke all the time."

"I'll quit," Roy responded meekly. "I'll quit just like I quit drinking and cursing."

Don paced the apartment in frustration.

"You're a hypocrite and a traitor to the family just like Dad! I've always tried to protect you. Why didn't you listen to me?"

"Because I was miserable, I guess," Roy replied. "I got convicted one night that keeping a lot of the Ten Commandments wasn't good enough. God finally got through to me that night. I realized that everything Dad had been saying was true. You know I never wanted to believe that stuff, Don. I counted the cost before I made the decision. But after I made it, I finally felt clean, loved, accepted and forgiven."

Don scowled, his scorn and rejection evident. His one ally in life had turned on him! Roy had joined the side of the enemy and now Don was clearly on his own. Dad had won; Don had lost and he felt totally isolated. *Nobody* understood him. His girlfriends abandoned him because they quickly saw that he was going no place in life. He failed at everything he did, and now he failed to protect his brother from the snares of his dad and Jesus!

"I won't preach at you," Roy said. "And I'm still human and I'll make lots of mistakes. But for the first time in my life I have peace. All I can say is that God has done something for me. I want Him to help you too, but I won't preach at you."

"I am the way." There was that nagging voice within Don again! Every now and then it shot through him like an arrow. Why did everything have to hit at once? What a rotten time for that voice to bug him! It seemed that *nobody* wanted Don Lessin to have any peace of mind. Everyone was against him. His total alienation in life enveloped him in a giant cloud of self-pity and gloom.

Roy began to read his Bible even in front of Don. Don tried to escape the agony of reality through heavier drinking. Many days he never got out of bed; the little he said was usually about the meaninglessness of life. His emptiness was at an all-time high.

Even his own family had nearly rejected him. He was that good-for-nothing who was going nowhere at age twenty-three. He had disappointed his mother and all his relatives with his behavior, lack of ambition and goals in life. Other sons were studying law or medicine, or entering business with their fathers. Not Don Lessin, however. He was caught on a hopeless treadmill of failure and rejection. Shrivelling up into his own private world, he shut out humanity. He drank to stifle his thoughts and fears, but still that nagging voice broke through all too often, short and simple and saying the same thing every time: *"I am the way."*

It was no small favor that Sarah continued to love Roy in spite of his new faith. She had the right to remain a Jew, but she was pleased that he had finally found peace. The family had not cut him off like he feared; even Don backed down from nagging at him.

In what appeared to be a last-ditch effort, Don determined to go off in search of the truth. He was wallowing in such personal misery that he allowed himself to entertain a new concept: perhaps the answers to life might rest with God after all. Not Jesus, but maybe God.

That inner voice spoke more frequently now. Had he totally flipped his mind? People who hear strange voices are generally locked away somewhere. Was Don a candidate for such an ignominious fate? Maybe he'd been drinking too much.

That voice again. It forced him to borrow a car and drive

straight to the Eagle Rock Covenant Church where his dad attended. As he sat in the church parking lot, he wondered if perhaps some time capsule had dropped him there. No, he willingly made the trip, in response to that voice which was nearly driving him crazy. He didn't have to accept a thing that would be said inside that freshly painted church building that Sunday night. He could sit in the last row of the church and walk out any time he wanted to. It was a free country and in spite of all his accusations against Christians, he was quite sure they wouldn't tie him in place and force the Bible down his throat!

But admittedly the cross on the front of the church was an obstacle to Don. He looked at it for several long moments as the congregation inside sang rousing songs that could be heard out in the parking lot. So many Jews had suffered because of that cross; there was still time to change his mind and back out of this whole idea. Nothing was forcing Don Lessin to enter that Gentile church. He could picture row after row of clean-cut looking Christians with, as he perceived it, painted-on smiles.

Nothing was forcing him, and yet something did. Against his better judgment, a magnetic pull drew him inside and he found himself sitting in the last pew looking at the backs of two hundred people—happy and enthusiastic people who seemed to have purpose and direction in life, at least from his vantage point.

What would his peers think? His Jewish friends would probably laugh him off the face of the earth. So what kind of purpose and direction did they have? Who knows, maybe some of them would be pleased that Don was finally making an attempt to get out of his pit.

He sat stiffly in the church pew in a quick-get-away position. Every muscle felt tense and awkward in such a strange setting. But slowly he began to relax as he sensed the atmosphere of love and acceptance in the church. The preacher radiated such a concern for his people. Don's preconceived notion that he might have walked into a lions' den vanished. He leaned back and breathed a noticeable sigh of relief—that is, until his dad turned around and spotted him. His surprise at

Don's presence was noticed by everyone.

Joe eagerly made his way to Don, trying to contain some of his joy over his son's presence. Immediately the walls went up again. Don's body stiffened and his face grew pained.

"Just leave me alone and let me work things out for myself," he whispered fiercely as Joe approached him. Joe nodded and turned away to leave the situation in God's hands. But tears rolled down his cheeks as he recognized the fact that God was, indeed, at work in this stubborn boy of his. Once again, his son was coming *to him* as the verse in Isaiah 60 had promised.

Don didn't want to listen to the preacher that night, but something wouldn't let him escape. The theme was familiar. He had heard it from his dad and had heard snatches of it on that Billy Graham telecast he had seen. For salvation, for peace with God, one had to commit his life to Jesus and be "born again." That sounds like reincarnation, Don thought. Faith in Jesus Christ is the only hope for a lost world going nowhere. Only God can give peace and purpose to the directionless. Don felt that was certainly a description of him. Only God can restore order out of chaos and bring joy out of mourning. Only Jesus offers eternal life. Nothing but faith in Jesus matters on God's scale of righteousness. Jesus is the way to a personal relationship with God. There were those words again: *"I am the way"*! Don did not understand much of the message, but he found himself agreeing with the pastor more than once.

He left before "the Christians could eat the lion," he thought grimly to himself, but he had to admit that he felt good about his visit. He decided to come back the following Sunday night. Those people had something he knew he needed. And even though Jesus would be preached again from that pulpit with a cross carved into its wood, Don intended to be back once more in the same spot.

The Hound of Heaven was on his trail; for the first time in his life, Don tried to outrun Him less frantically.

Don kept his secret pursuit to himself, not even sharing it with Roy who was now making plans to attend Bible school in

168

Minnesota. But for three Sunday evenings he made the trip to Eagle Rock; he allowed himself to lower the barriers enough to receive from the pastor and people. Many reached out to him in a kind of a love he didn't know existed. He felt it was unconditional, asking for nothing in return, even his soul. Consistently they gave, cared and shared. He felt they would love him even if he remained steeped in his sin. He had ridiculed people like this most of his adult life; in fact, he was still skeptical. But in spite of his antagonism, they continued to show their love for him.

Their consistent patience with him gave the message great credibility with Don. He was convinced after three visits to the church that they loved him as an individual and not as a spiritual statistic.

His defenses were further broken down and his anger subsided. The spiritual longing in his heart grew, and that inner voice spoke to him even more. Don recognized that God was beginning to break through his stiff-necked exterior.

He stumbled home in the predawn darkness from his job at the flower market. Maybe it was merely his fatigue, but he felt that he was left defenseless, without argument or excuse, before God. He sat glassy-eyed in the living room of their apartment. Roy was asleep in another room; he had kept his promise to Don to not preach at him. And yet no one knew better than Don how radically his brother's life had changed since he "gave his life to Christ," as Roy put it. Roy had been able to clean up his way of living. He had quit smoking and drinking almost overnight "through the power of the Lord," as Joe had explained it. Externally Don had rolled with laughter but inwardly he admitted that it was impressive.

Jesus is the way. There it was again—that voice.

He shook himself from a stupor and paced the apartment. Could Jesus *really* be the way? Could Don, a Jew, really accept that? So many other voices wanted to repudiate the whole concept that Jesus is the Son of God, the Savior and Messiah of mankind. And yet what did he have to lose—except a little pride—if he should ask God, or Jesus, to come into his life? Nobody would have to know that Don Lessin had prayed to Jesus, only to discover that Jesus was a hoax, a lie perpetrated for centuries by zealous but deluded Christians. And there was an outside chance, slim to be sure, that everything those Christians had preached was true.

So how does one pray? How does one properly address God—or Jesus? Don suddenly remembered the time back in the Army when he prayed and his toothache mysteriously disappeared. Was that the grace of God manifested through answered prayer like Joe had insisted? Don had prayed such a *simple* prayer that time, and yet maybe God had heard him. Maybe God wasn't caught up in eloquent prayers; maybe he should try a simple prayer again.

Only an outdoor street light shone into the apartment as he got down on his knees. He felt terribly foolish and groped for the right words.

"If everything my dad says is true, show me, God." Then he paused and said once again, more loudly, *"Show me."*

He waited.

"And if Jesus is real, and if I can experience His peace, show me that, too. I want to know you, and I want that peace. Just show me."

Nothing happened. He got up off his knees and waited for some exhilarated feeling. His dad had said that when one is "born again," he knows it! It is a personal experience between God and man, and God lets us know when we've entered into that relationship with Him.

So why had nothing changed? Maybe he had turned off his feelings so long ago that he couldn't even feel toward God, or feel God reaching toward him. Then again, maybe he had said the wrong words; or worse, maybe God wanted nothing to do with Don Lessin. Perhaps God simply hadn't heard his prayer because He had turned a deaf ear to him.

Don went to his bed and stared at the ceiling for three hours as the dawn began to break. Somewhere during that three-hour period gentle waves of peace began to envelope him. He felt as if a giant weight was being removed from him. A surge of inner joy followed. Then in the stillness of his room, with the sounds of the distant rumble of traffic, he heard that voice again! It said something different this time, however.

"Now you belong to me, Don."

Every ounce of skepticism in him wanted to refute this whole experience! But it was real and not imagined. It was from God, and not the mind-games of an overly tired loser who wanted religion as another crutch. He felt an inner assurance that God and man had communicated and that a worthless, undirected sinner was now safely in the hands of the living God, who henceforth would order Don's footsteps.

He sat on the edge of his bed. How should he tell the world what had happened to him tonight? Most of them would dish out the same ridicule he had given his dad. He previously had agreed with them that one's life is changed by making it big in life, by having a lot of girlfriends or maybe by marrying a real knock-out; but it is *not* altered through a simple prayer! And yet he *knew* his life had just been transformed! He simply *knew* it!

He decided he would begin by telling Roy, who was already up, studying at the kitchen table. So how do you tell your kid brother that you were wrong? Don's stoic self wanted to be casual, and yet with the weight of guilt off him, he felt he really should do childish cartwheels down the street.

Don realized that a whole new feeling was welling up inside him—love. He wanted more than anything to go over to his mother's and tell her how much he loved her! He had never been able to do that before. He wanted to tell her how sorry he was for all the years of heartache he had caused her.

And he had a new appreciation of his dad and all Joe had gone through. Joe had prayed and agonized over his boys for so many years. The whole family had rejected him. Yet he never gave up but went right on loving "with the love of Jesus," as Joe put it. His dad's patience and long-suffering overwhelmed Don.

He left his room in search of Roy. For several moments he paced back and forth behind Roy, who was sitting with an open Bible at the table. The tough guy, Don, suddenly had to come on meekly, had to humble himself and admit that he'd been wrong. Since Don never had any practice at that, it was awkward, to say the least.

He cleared his throat. "Roy, I've made a decision. For Jesus, that is."

Roy closed his Bible and turned to face Don. There were a few seconds as each groped for words. Tears and emotions had never come easily to either of them, and yet this seemed to be an appropriate occasion for both.

Roy reached out his hand to his brother.

"Welcome, Don. Welcome to the family of God."

Joe Lessin had prayed for his sons for ten years. He had despaired more than once that God might not be able to answer those prayers, because he had seen little change in their lives.

But God had been faithful to Joe, for his sons had, indeed, come to him from afar.

Epilogue

People worldwide have been touched by God's love through the lives of Joe, Don, and Roy. God planted a seed the day Joe discovered the Bible, and it has sprouted into a tree deeply rooted in His mercy.

Joe has pastored, taught, and counseled in the ministry for nearly forty years. During some of those years, he returned to his first occupation: peddling! Selling general merchandise from a green van, Joe shared the gospel with many people along his route. Now 82, Joe actively serves the Lord at the Fair Havens Ministry Center in California.

Don became a missionary to Mexico in 1964, and spent many years in the dry climate of the north pastoring and helping establish churches. He now pastors a large-town church in the central part of the country.

Roy, after spending several years as a missionary in Puerto Rico and Mexico, co-founded Outreach Publications in 1971. For twenty years, he wrote much of the copy found on the company's DaySpring greeting cards. Millions of people have been blessed by his writing. Currently, Roy writes and develops product exclusively for Best To You, the catalog division of Outreach Publications.